Garlic

A Simple Garlic Cookbook for Everyone

By
BookSumo Press

Published by
http://www.booksumo.com

ENJOY THE RECIPES?
KEEP ON COOKING
WITH 6 MORE FREE COOKBOOKS!

Visit our website and simply enter your email address to join the club and receive your 6 cookbooks.

LEGAL NOTES

Table of Contents

Creamy Crushed Tomato Soup Bowls 9

Hot Carrot Mash 10

Basil and Ginger Basmati 11

Fried Fish with Honey Garlic Basmati 12

Algerian Weeknight Dinner 13

Tomato Braised Egg Skillet 14

Algerian Chicken Hot Pot 15

North African Style Carrots 16

Tomato Based Chicken and Chickpeas 17

Algerian Saffron Bowls 18

Baked Chicken Oran 19

Couscous Ghardaïa 20

Myriam's Salad 21

How to Make Haricot Beans 22

Algerian Style Lamb and Beans 23

Green Bean Bowls 24

Hot Broad Beans 25

Aunty's Beef Stew 26

Lulu's Oven Tagine 27

Hot Minty Carrots 28

Buttery Lentil Bowls 29

Algerian Soup Pot 30

North African Eggplants 31

Handmade Pasta with Sauce 32

Carrot and Celery Soup 34

Dolmas Biskra 35

African Tuna Sandwiches with Handmade Bread 37

Chili Sausage and Potato Stew 39

Algerian Lamb Shoulder 40

Lamb Tagine with Saffron 41

Arabian Meatball Soup 42

Whole Chicken Mediterranean Style 44

Mint and Tomato Lentils with Lamb 45

Garlicky Lamb 46

Fathia's Bean Bowls 47

Algerian Mash for Toast 48

North African Frittatas 49

Semolina Bread with Chili Spread 50

Grilled Salad 51

Mendoza Kabobs 52

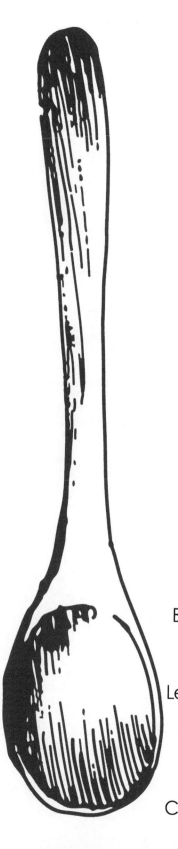

Grilled Gazebo Salad 53

Southwest Rib-Eye Steaks 54

A Whole Chicken in Belize 55

Topped Seafood Tacos 56

Garlicky Fish Griller 57

Honey Basil Chicken 58

Hot Jamaican Filets 59

Southwest Sirloin 60

Blackened Chicken Cutlets 61

Grilled Bread 62

Fish Africano 63

How to Braise Brussel Sprouts 64

Red Bell Brussel Sprouts 65

Lover's Brussel Sprouts 66

Thai Style Brussel Sprouts 67

Brussel Sprouts with Cannellini 68

Backyard Brussel Sprouts 69

Lemony Agave Brussel Sprouts 70

Waldorf Brussel Sprouts 71

Full Barcelona Ceviche 72

Catalina's Cabbage Ceviche 73

Ceviche Brasileiro 74

Country Ceviche 75

Southwest Ceviche 76

Bethany Beach Ceviche 77

Cinco De Mayo Chili 78

Saturday Night Texan Rice 79

Traditional Mexican Spicy Vermicelli 80

Mexican Cheese Dumplings 81

Mexico City-San Antonio Pierogies 82

San Luis Salmon 84

Caribbean x Mexican Chuck Roast 85

Real Authentic Tamales 86

Fresh Green Enchiladas 88

Red, White, and Green Soup 90

Tampico Inspired Meal Pie 91

Spicy Honey Tilapia Tacos 92

Mexican Skillet 94

Chipotle Veggies & Black-Eyed Peas 95

Cheesy Chipotle Lamb Burgers in Maple Glaze 96

Hot Chipotle Peach Salsa 97

Beef Brisket in Chipotle Gravy 98

Classic Teriyaki Sauce 99

Classic Teriyaki Chuck Burgers 100

Teriyaki Chicken Thighs 101

Teriyaki Penne 102

Tropical Teriyaki Kabobs 103

Teriyaki Steak BBQ 104

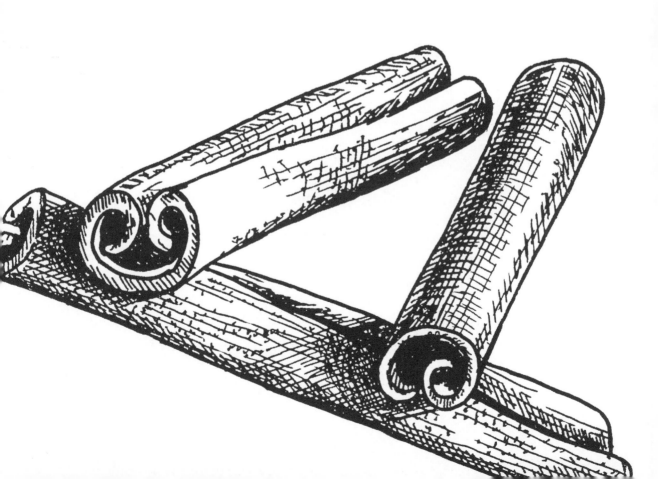

Creamy Crushed Tomato Soup Bowls

🍲 Prep Time: 15 mins

🕐 Total Time: 1 hr 15 mins

Servings per Recipe: 6
Calories	237.8
Fat	4.0g
Cholesterol	0.0mg
Sodium	1203.8mg
Carbohydrates	43.5g
Protein	10.4g

Ingredients

1 C. lentils, sorted & rinsed
1 cinnamon stick
7 C. water
1 tbsp olive oil
3 C. minced onions
2 tbsp minced garlic
2 tsp salt
1 tsp turmeric
1 1/2 tsp cumin seeds
2 tsp ground cumin

3 bay leaves
1 (28 oz.) cans crushed tomatoes
2 C. cooked chickpeas, drained and rinsed
black pepper
cayenne pepper
currants
plain yogurt
parsley, chopped
fresh mint, chopped

Directions

1. Place a large pot over medium heat. Stir in it the cinnamon stick with lentils, 7 C. of water and a pinch of salt.

2. Cook them until they start boiling. Lower the heat and put on the lid. Cook them for an extra 32 min.

3. Once the time is up, discard the cinnamon stick. Strain the lentils. Place the cooking liquid aside.

4. Place a stew pot over medium heat. Heat in it the oil.

5. Cook in it the onion, garlic, salt, turmeric, cumin seeds, ground cumin, and bay leaves for 8 min.

6. Stir in the tomatoes and cook them until they start boiling. Lower the heat and put on half a cover. Let it cook for 16 min.

7. Add the lentils with chickpeas. Cook them for 6 min. Fold the lemon juice with a pinch of salt and pepper.

8. Serve your soup hot. Enjoy.

HOT
Carrot Mash

 Prep Time: 20 mins

Total Time: 35 mins

Servings per Recipe: 4
Calories	205.8
Fat	14.2g
Cholesterol	0.0mg
Sodium	720.5mg
Carbohydrates	19.7g
Protein	2.0g

Ingredients

1 3/4 lbs. carrots, peeled and chopped
1 tsp salt
1/4 C. olive oil
3 tbsp white wine vinegar
1 garlic clove, crushed
1 tsp harissa

2 tsp cumin, ground
black olives

Directions

1. Place a large salted saucepan of water over medium heat. Bring it to a boil.
2. Cook in it the carrots until they become soft. Drain them and mash them with a food processor or potato masher.
3. Get a mixing bowl: Combine in it the mashed carrots with olive oil, vinegar, garlic, seasoning, and harissa.
4. Adjust the seasoning of your carrot mash then serve it with some toast.
5. Enjoy.

Basil
and Ginger Basmati

Prep Time: 15 mins
Total Time: 45 mins

Servings per Recipe: 4	
Calories	197.6
Fat	3.7g
Cholesterol	0.0mg
Sodium	280.0mg
Carbohydrates	36.6g
Protein	4.2g

Ingredients

1 C. basmati rice, rinsed and drained
2 tsp canola oil
2 tsp minced peeled ginger
2 garlic cloves, minced
2 1/4 C. fat-free chicken broth
1 tbsp chopped basil

2 tsp chopped mint
1/4 tsp black pepper

Directions

1. Set your oven to 350 degrees F before doing anything else.
2. In a large pan, heat the oil over medium-high heat and sauté the garlic and ginger for about 30 seconds.
3. Stir in the rice and cook for about 1 minute, stirring continuously.
4. Stir in the remaining ingredients and bring to a boil.
5. Cover the pan and cook in the oven for about 25 minutes, stirring once.
6. Remove from the oven and with a fork, fluff the rice.
7. Serve hot.

FRIED FISH
with Honey Garlic Basmati

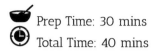

Prep Time: 30 mins
Total Time: 40 mins

Servings per Recipe: 2
Calories	915.9
Fat	61.6g
Cholesterol	15.2mg
Sodium	2068.0mg
Carbohydrates	83.4g
Protein	9.6g

Ingredients

Dressing
1 tbsp chopped cilantro
1 tbsp chopped green onion
1 tbsp grated ginger
1 tbsp sliced shallot
1 1/2 tsp chopped garlic
1/2 tsp black sesame seeds
1/2 tsp white sesame seeds
1 tbsp red chili paste
2 tbsp honey
1/4 C. rice vinegar
1/4 C. soy sauce
1/2 C. canola oil
Fish
1/4 C. all-purpose flour
1/4 C. cornstarch
salt
ground black pepper
2 butterflied skin-on rainbow trout
vegetable oil
1 1/2 C. cooked basmati rice
1 tsp chopped basil
1/4 tsp chopped thyme
1/4 tsp chopped oregano
1 tbsp butter
cilantro stem

Directions

1. For the vinaigrette: in a bowl, add the shallots, green onions, garlic, ginger, cilantro, sesame seeds, honey, chile paste, vinegar, oil and soy sauce and beat until well combined.

2. For the trout and rice: in a shallow bowl, mix together the cornstarch, flour, 1 1/2 tsp of the salt and 1 tsp of the black pepper.

3. Coat the trout fillets with the flour mixture evenly.

4. In a large skillet, heat about 1/8-inch of the oil over medium-high heat.

5. Place the trout, skin side down and fry about 2 minutes per side.

6. Meanwhile, in another skillet, mix together the butter, rice, fresh herbs, salt and pepper and cook for about 5 minutes, stirring frequently.

7. place the rice mixture in the center of 2 serving plates and top with the trout.

8. Drizzle the vinaigrette around the rice and serve immediately with a garnishing of the cilantro sprigs.

Algerian
Weeknight Dinner (Spicy Ground Beef with Beans)

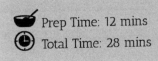 Prep Time: 12 mins

Total Time: 28 mins

Servings per Recipe: 6

Calories	217.0
Fat	8.2g
Cholesterol	49.1mg
Sodium	633.8mg
Carbohydrates	16.6g
Protein	18.4g

Ingredients

1 lb lean ground beef
1 1/2 C. onions, chopped
1 C. green bell pepper, chopped
3 garlic cloves, crushed
8 oz. kidney beans
8 oz. hominy
1 tsp. salt
1 tsp. dried basil

1/2 tsp. ground black pepper
1/4 tsp. sugar
1/4 tsp. dried oregano
1/4 tsp. red pepper flakes
2 C. water

Directions

1. Place a large pan over medium heat. Cook in it the beef with onion, garlic and bell pepper for 7 min.
2. Drain them and discard the excess grease. Pour them back into the pan.
3. Add the kidney beans, hominy, salt, basil, pepper, sugar, oregano and red pepper flakes.
4. Stir in 2 C. of water. Let them cook over medium heat until the stew becomes thick for at least 10 to 12 min.
5. Serve it hot with some rice.
6. Enjoy.

TOMATO
Braised Egg Skillet (Shakshouka I)

 Prep Time: 10 mins
Total Time: 30 mins

Servings per Recipe: 4
Calories	252.8
Fat	15.5g
Cholesterol	186.0mg
Sodium	85.8mg
Carbohydrates	20.5g
Protein	9.4g

Ingredients

3 tbsp. olive oil
1/2 tsp. cumin seed
1 tbsp. paprika
1 onion, thinly sliced
1 tbsp. harissa, for a spicier, deeper flavor
2-3 garlic cloves, minced
3 tomatoes, peeled, seeded and diced
1 potato, small diced cubes
1 green bell pepper, diced
1 red bell pepper, diced
1 yellow bell pepper, diced, if not using add more red and green bell pepper

1-2 chili pepper, for those that like heat
1 C. water
kosher salt
fresh ground pepper
4 eggs
parsley or cilantro, chopped
black olives
capers

Directions

1. Place a large pan over medium heat. Heat in it the oil.
2. Cook in it the cumin seeds for 20 sec. Add the paprika and cook them for 10 sec.
3. Stir in the garlic with the onion and cook them for 6 min.
4. Stir in the tomato and cook them until they start simmering. Stir in the peppers with potato, water, salt, and pepper.
5. Lower the heat and put on the lid. Cook them for 12 min while adding more water if needed.
6. Once the time is up, crack the eggs on top and put on the lid. Cook them for 10 to 12 min until they are done.
7. Serve your chakchouka pan hot with some bread.
8. Enjoy.

Algerian
Chicken Hot Pot

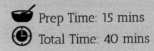 Prep Time: 15 mins

Total Time: 40 mins

Servings per Recipe: 6
Calories	230.8
Fat	5.1g
Cholesterol	35.0mg
Sodium	816.1mg
Carbohydrates	26.6g
Protein	19.9g

Ingredients

3 C. chicken broth
1 chicken bouillon cube
2 C. cooked chicken, chopped
1 medium onion, chopped
2 C. fresh green beans, cut
2 carrots, sliced
1 tsp. ground cumin
1 tsp. basil
1 garlic clove, minced
2 bay leaves

1/2 tsp. dried parsley
salt
pepper
2 medium tomatoes, chopped
2 small zucchini, sliced (or 1 medium)
1 (16 oz.) cans garbanzo beans, drained
1/4 tsp. ground red pepper

Directions

1. Place a saucepan over medium heat. Combine in it the broth, bouillon, chopped chicken, onion, green beans, carrots, cumin, basil, garlic, bay leaves, parsley, salt, and pepper.
2. Heat them until they start boiling. Lower the heat and put on the lid. Cook them for 8 to 9 min.
3. Stir in the zucchini with tomatoes and cook them for 4 min.
4. Stir in the red pepper with garbanzo beans. Put on the lid and heat them for 3 to 5 min.
5. Adjust the seasoning of your stew then serve it.
6. Enjoy.

NORTH AFRICAN STYLE
Carrots

Prep Time: 10 mins
Total Time: 40 mins

Servings per Recipe: 4
Calories	148.2
Fat	10.6g
Cholesterol	0.0mg
Sodium	87.1mg
Carbohydrates	13.1g
Protein	1.4g

Ingredients

17.6 oz.. Carrots, peeled and sliced
3 tbsp. oil
3 garlic cloves, minced
1 hot pepper
1/2 tsp. caraway seed
1 tsp. paprika

1 1/2 tbsp. vinegar
salt and black pepper

Directions

1. Bring a large salted saucepan of water to a boil. Cook in it the carrots for 10 to 14 until they become soft.
2. Combine the garlic with hot pepper, red pepper, caraway seeds and salt. Grind them until they become like a paste.
3. Transfer the mixture to a mixing bowl. Stir into it 1 tbsp. of water with oil. Mix them well.
4. Drain the carrots and transfer them to a skillet. Pour over them the pepper sauce and put on the lid.
5. Cook them for 3 to 4 min then serve them warm.
6. Enjoy.

Tomato Based Chicken and Chickpeas

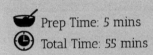 Prep Time: 5 mins

Total Time: 55 mins

Servings per Recipe: 4

Calories	219.0
Fat	4.0g
Cholesterol	7.2mg
Sodium	664.6mg
Carbohydrates	34.2g
Protein	11.5g

Ingredients

8 chicken pieces
1 small onion, Chopped
4 garlic cloves, crushed
1/2 tsp. ras el hanout spice mix
1/4 tsp. harissa
2 allspice berries

2 tsp. tomato paste
400 g chickpeas, drained
2 pints chicken stock

Directions

1. Place a large saucepan over medium heat. Heat in it 2 tbsp. of oil.

2. Brown in it the chicken pieces for 4 to 5 min on each side.

3. Stir in the garlic, spices, salt, tomato puree and Harissa. Let them cook for 2 to 3 min.

4. Stir in the stock and heat them until they start boiling.

5. Lower the heat and let them cook for 32 min.

6. Stir in the chickpeas and cook them for 10 to 12 min until the stew becomes thick.

7. Adjust the seasoning of your stew then serve it.

8. Enjoy.

ALGERIAN
Saffron Bowls

Prep Time: 10 mins
Total Time: 1 hr 3 mins

Servings per Recipe: 4

Calories	420.5
Fat	21.7g
Cholesterol	152.9mg
Sodium	715.0mg
Carbohydrates	6.3g
Protein	49.2g

Ingredients

2 tbsp. olive oil
2 lbs. boneless skinless chicken breasts, cubed
1 tbsp. butter
4 garlic cloves, minced
1 tsp. saffron, crumbled
1 bunch cilantro, finely chopped

1 C. water
8 oz. kalamata olives, pitted
1 lemon, juiced
salt & freshly ground black pepper

Directions

1. Place a large pot over high heat. Heat in it the oil.
2. Cook in it the chicken cubes for 10 to 12 while stirring all the time.
3. Add the butter, garlic, saffron, and cilantro. Cook them for 12 min while stirring often.
4. Stir in the water and heat them until they start boiling.
5. Lower the heat and cook them for 26 min. add the lemon juice with olives.
6. Cook them for 10 min. adjust the seasoning of your stew then serve it hot with some couscous.
7. Enjoy.

Baked Chicken Oran

🥣 Prep Time: 20 mins
🕐 Total Time: 2 hrs

Servings per Recipe: 4

Calories	562.1
Fat	43.5g
Cholesterol	183.3mg
Sodium	2767.6mg
Carbohydrates	3.3g
Protein	38.1g

Ingredients

1 (3-4 lb) roasting chicken
2 lemons, halved
2 large garlic cloves, minced
3 tbsp. unsalted butter
1 tbsp. seasoning, mixed
1 1/2 tbsp. coarse salt

coarse salt
fresh ground pepper
olive oil
3-4 sprigs thyme

Directions

1. Before you do anything, preheat the oven to 450 F.
2. Arrange the chicken on a roasting dish. Reach under the skin to loosen it without tearing it.
3. Combine the garlic with salt in a mortar. Use a pestle to mince until it becomes like a paste.
4. Add the butter with spices and mix them well with your hands.
5. Spread the mixture all over the chicken while reaching under the skin.
6. Drizzle the lemon juice all over it then season it with some salt and pepper.
7. Stuff the chicken cavity with thyme and lemon halves.
8. Place it in the oven with the breast facing down. Roast it for 16 min.
9. Lower the oven temperature to 350 F.
10. Flip the chicken and roast it for 1 h 30 min until it becomes golden brown while basting it with some olive oil.
11. Once the time is up, drain the chicken and wrap it in a piece of foil.
12. Let it rest for 5 min then serve it.
13. Enjoy.

COUSCOUS
Ghardaïa

Prep Time: 15 mins
Total Time: 30 mins

Servings per Recipe: 6
Calories	226.4
Fat	5.6g
Cholesterol	1.5mg
Sodium	86.0mg
Carbohydrates	38.6g
Protein	6.9g

Ingredients

2 tbsp. olive oil
1 medium onion, chopped
8 oz. mushrooms, sliced
1 grated carrot
2 garlic cloves, minced
1/2 tsp. cumin
1/2 tsp. ground coriander

1 lemon, zest of
1 lemon, juice of
1/2 C. raisins
1 1/4 C. chicken stock
1 C. couscous

Directions

1. Place a large skillet over medium heat. Heat in it the oil.
2. Cook in it the onion with carrots and mushrooms for 5 min.
3. Stir in the seasonings with lemon zest, raisins, and couscous. Cook them for 2 min.
4. Stir in the lemon juice with stock. Lower the heat and cook them for 3 to 4 min.
5. Put on the lid and turn off the heat. Let it sit for 5 to 6 min. Serve it warm.
6. Enjoy.

Myriam's
Salad

Prep Time: 10 mins
Total Time: 50 mins

Servings per Recipe: 2
Calories	93.4
Fat	2.9g
Cholesterol	0.0mg
Sodium	14.1mg
Carbohydrates	16.7g
Protein	3.2g

Ingredients

3 large green bell peppers
2 vine ripened tomatoes
1-2 garlic clove, minced
2-3 tbsp. water
1 tsp. olive oil

salt
vinegar

Directions

1. Place the bell peppers on the stove and grill them until they become black.
2. Transfer them to a plastic bag and seal it. Let it rest for 5 to 6 min.
3. Once the time is up, peel them, rinse them and chop them.
4. Place a skillet over medium heat. Heat in it the oil.
5. Stir in it the tomatoes with peppers and garlic. Cook them for 3 min.
6. Stir in a pinch of salt and cook them for 16 min while often stirring.
7. Serve your tomato salad warm.
8. Enjoy.

HOW TO MAKE
Haricot Beans

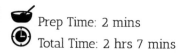
Prep Time: 2 mins
Total Time: 2 hrs 7 mins

Servings per Recipe: 6
Calories	107.2
Fat	9.7g
Cholesterol	0.0mg
Sodium	984.0mg
Carbohydrates	5.4g
Protein	1.3g

Ingredients

17.5 oz. dried haricot beans, soaked overnight
12 C. water
6 1/2 tsp. paprika
3 1/2 tsp. ground cumin
14 oz. cans plum tomatoes, pureed
6 garlic cloves, minced

6 - 8 pieces chicken
4 tbsp. olive oil
1 pinch black pepper
2 1/2 tsp. salt
olive oil, & vinegar to serve

Directions

1. Place a large pot over medium heat.
2. Stir in it the beans with olive oil, meat paprika, and cumin. Cook them for 4 min.
3. Add to them 8 1/2 C. of water with a pinch of salt and pepper. Put on the lid and bring them to a simmer.
4. Lower the heat and cook them for 60 min.
5. Add 2 C. of water with tomatoes, garlic, 2 tsp. salt, 2 1/2 tsp. paprika and 1 1/2 tsp. cumin.
6. Put on the lid and let them cook for 30 to 35 min.
7. Once the time is up, remove the cover and let it cook for an extra 30 to 35 min.
8. Stir in the vinegar with olive oil then serve them warm.
9. Enjoy.

Algerian Style
Lamb and Beans

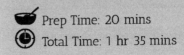 Prep Time: 20 mins

Total Time: 1 hr 35 mins

Servings per Recipe: 8
Calories	125.2
Fat	2.5g
Cholesterol	68.9mg
Sodium	61.9mg
Carbohydrates	16.0g
Protein	10.4g

Ingredients

1 lb. tripe or 1 lb. lamb, if preferred, diced
4 yellow onions, chopped
2-4 cloves garlic, minced
2 green peppers
1/2 tsp. black pepper
2 tsp. cumin
1 tsp. paprika

1 C. white beans, soaked for at least 2 hours
salt
4 tbsp. chopped cilantro
2 tomatoes, chopped

Directions

1. Place the peppers on the grill and cook them until they become black.
2. Transfer them to a plastic bag and seal it. Let them sit for 15 min.
3. Once the time is up, peel them, rinse them and dice them.
4. Place a large skillet over medium heat. Heat in it a splash of oil.
5. Brown in it the lamb dices for 3 min. Place it aside.
6. Add the onion with garlic, green peppers, and 3 tbsp. of olive oil.
7. Stir in the seasonings and cook them for 2 min. Stir in the meat and cook them for 2 min.
8. Add enough water to cover them and heat them until they start boiling.
9. Bring them to a rolling boil for 60 min.
10. Once the time is up, stir in the tomato and cook them for 20 min over low heat.
11. Add the white beans and heat them through.
12. Adjust the seasoning of your stew then serve it hot.
13. Enjoy.

GREEN BEAN
Bowls

Prep Time: 10 mins
Total Time: 50 mins

Servings per Recipe: 4
Calories	141.0
Fat	11.6g
Cholesterol	0.0mg
Sodium	22.0mg
Carbohydrates	8.9g
Protein	2.6g

Ingredients

1 lb. green beans, clean and trim
4 C. water
3 tbsp. oil
1 garlic clove, mashed
1/2 tsp. cumin, ground
1/2 tsp. paprika

1/4 tsp. clove, ground
1 tbsp. almonds, slivered

Directions

1. Bring a large saucepan of salted water to a boil over high heat.
2. Cook in it the beans for 32 min. Drain it and transfer it to a saucepan.
3. Add the oil, garlic, cumin, paprika, and cloves. Cook them for 3 min.
4. Stir in the almonds and toss them to coat. Stir in the green beans and adjust their seasoning.
5. Adjust the seasoning of your salad then serve it.
6. Enjoy.

Hot
Broad Beans

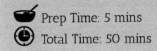 Prep Time: 5 mins

Total Time: 50 mins

Servings per Recipe: 4	
Calories	277.7
Fat	10.8g
Cholesterol	0.0mg
Sodium	1140.1mg
Carbohydrates	33.1g
Protein	14.2g

Ingredients

2 1/4 lb broad bean in the pod, trimmed and bite-size pieces
1 bunch fresh cilantro, chopped
6 garlic cloves, peeled and minced
3-4 tbsp olive oil
1 tsp. paprika
1/4 tsp. cayenne

1/8 tsp. black pepper
salt (1/2 tsp. minimum)
1-1 1/2 tsp. vinegar
600 ml water

Directions

1. Place a large pot over medium heat. Heat in it the oil.
2. Cook in it the garlic with beans for 3 min. Stir in the remaining ingredients and put on the lid.
3. Cook them for 26 to 32 min until the sauce becomes thick. Serve it hot.
4. Enjoy.

AUNTY'S
Beef Stew

Prep Time: 20 mins
Total Time: 1 hr 35 mins

Servings per Recipe: 6
Calories   564.0
Fat   27.4g
Cholesterol   50.6mg
Sodium   751.5mg
Carbohydrates   54.7g
Protein   26.6g

Ingredients

1/4 cup olive oil
1 lb. stewing beef, cubed
2 medium onions, chopped
4 garlic cloves, crushed
1/2 cup chopped cilantro leaf
1 hot pepper, of your choice, chopped
38 ounces canned chickpeas, undrained
4 medium tomatoes, diced
1/4 tsp pepper

1/2 tsp cumin
1/2 tsp thyme
2 cups low sodium chicken broth
salt
1/4 cup green olives, pitted and chopped
2 tbsps lemon juice

Directions

1. Place a stew pot over medium heat. Heat in it the oil. Brown in it the beef for 4 min.
2. Stir in the hot pepper with onion, and cilantro. Cook them for 3 min.
3. Stir in the garlic with a pinch of salt. Cook them for 4 min.
4. Add the tomatoes with chickpeas, thyme, pepper, cumin, broth, a pinch of salt and pepper.
5. Cook them until they start boiling. Put on the lid and lower the heat.
6. Let them cook for 60 min. Add the lemon juice with green olives. Let them cook for an extra 6 min.
7. Serve your stew warm with some bread.
8. Enjoy.

Lulu's
Oven Tagine

🍲 Prep Time: 30 mins

🕐 Total Time: 1 hr

Servings per Recipe: 4

Calories	445.4
Fat	27.0g
Cholesterol	399.2mg
Sodium	567.3mg
Carbohydrates	27.0g
Protein	23.9g

Ingredients

6 eggs, raw
2 eggs, hard-boiled, peeled and chopped
1 tomatoes, deseeded and chopped
1/2 onion, chopped
1 - 2 garlic clove, chopped
1 chili pepper, chopped
2 - 3 potatoes, peeled and chopped
1/2 cup parsley, chopped
6 ounces cheese, grated
1 1/2 cups ground meat

Spices
cumin
turmeric
coriander seeds
harissa
salt and pepper
Oil
2 tbsps vegetable oil

Directions

1. Place a large pan over medium heat. Heat in it the oil.
2. Cook in it the potatoes with turmeric, cumin, a pinch of salt and pepper for 4 min. Stir in the onion with meat. Cook them for 3 min. Stir in the harissa with garlic, chili pepper and a splash of water.
3. Let them cook for another 3 min. Stir in the parsley with cheese, tomato, and chopped eggs then turn off the heat.
4. Get a mixing bowl: Whisk in it 6 eggs with a pinch of salt and pepper.
5. Add it to the potato mixture and combine them well. Spoon the mixture into a greased casserole dish.
6. Sprinkle the cheese on top. Bake it for 25 to 32 min. Serve it warm.
7. Enjoy.

HOT
Minty Carrots

 Prep Time: 5 mins

Total Time: 20 mins

Servings per Recipe: 4

Calories	189.8
Fat	7.7g
Cholesterol	0.0mg
Sodium	505.7mg
Carbohydrates	30.2g
Protein	3.1g

Ingredients

2 1/2 lbs. carrots, peeled and sliced
1/2 tsp. hot sauce
2 tbsp. light olive oil
3 garlic cloves, sliced thinly
1 lemon, juice of
2 tsp. cumin seeds, toasted
1/2 tsp. sugar

1/2 tsp. salt
2 tbsp. mint, finely chopped

Directions

1. Prepare a steamer. Cook in it the carrots for 5 to 6 min until they become slightly soft.
2. Place them aside along with 5 tbsp. of the steaming water.
3. Place a pan over medium heat. Toast in it the cumin seeds for 1 min. Place them aside.
4. Place a stew pot over medium heat. Heat in it the oil. Cook in it the carrots for 1 to 2 min.
5. Stir in the steaming water with hot sauce, lemon juice, cumin seed, sugar, and salt.
6. Toss them to coat. Stir in the carrots and put on half a cover.
7. Let them cook 8 to 10 min until they become soft.
8. Add the mint leaves and serve them right away.
9. Enjoy.

Buttery
Lentil Bowls

🥣 Prep Time: 20 mins
🕐 Total Time: 3 hrs 20 mins

Servings per Recipe: 6

Calories	391.4
Fat	15.5g
Cholesterol	58.6mg
Sodium	1096.5mg
Carbohydrates	31.7g
Protein	29.5g

Ingredients

2 tbsp. olive oil
1 lb. lean lamb, cut into 1/2- 3/4 inch cubes
salt, to taste
pepper, to taste
8 C. chicken broth
1 C. lentils, soaked for 2 h and drained
1 medium onion, minced

1 carrot, scraped, and finely chopped
1 garlic clove, minced
2 tbsp. butter
1/4 tsp. cumin
1/4 tsp. cinnamon
1 C. orzo pasta

Directions

1. Place a pot over medium heat. Heat in it the oil.
2. Brown in it the lamb pieces with a pinch of salt and pepper for 4 min.
3. Stir in half of the broth and put on the lid. Cook them for 30 to 35 min until the meat becomes tender.
4. Add the rest of the broth with lentils. Cook them for 16 min.
5. Place a large pan over medium heat. Heat in it the butter until it melts.
6. Cook in it the garlic with carrot and onion for 3 min. Transfer it to the lamb pot with orzo.
7. Put on half a lid and let them cook for 10 to 12 min until the lentils and meat are done.
8. Adjust the seasoning of your soup then serve it hot.
9. Enjoy.

ALGERIAN
Soup Pot

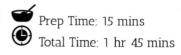 Prep Time: 15 mins

Total Time: 1 hr 45 mins

Servings per Recipe: 6

Calories	264.7
Fat	8.5g
Cholesterol	34.6mg
Sodium	619.0mg
Carbohydrates	30.9g
Protein	16.3g

Ingredients

1-2 tbsp olive oil
3-4 chicken drumsticks
1 large onion, finely chopped
2-3 garlic cloves, minced
4 tsp. ras el hanout spice mix
1/2 tsp. ginger
1/2 tsp. turmeric
1/4 tsp. cinnamon
3/4 tsp. sweet paprika
4 C. chicken stock

4 C. water
17.5 oz. canned chick-peas
14 oz. chopped canned tomatoes
1/4 preserved lemon, very finely chopped
1/4 C. fresh cilantro, chopped
1/2 lemon, juice of

Directions

1. Place a large pot over medium heat. Heat in it the oil.
2. Cook in it the chicken drumsticks until they become golden brown. Drain them and place them aside.
3. Stir the spices into the same pan and cook them for few seconds. Stir in back the chicken with onion, preserved lemon, garlic, stock, and water.
4. Cook them until they start boiling. Lower the heat and put on the lid. Cook them for 60 min.
5. Drain the chicken drumsticks, shred them and add them to the pot. Stir the chickpeas with tomato and cook them for 22 min.
6. Once the time is up, add the preserved lemon with cilantro, lemon juice, and cilantro.
7. Adjust the seasoning of your soup then serve hot.
8. Enjoy.

North African Eggplants

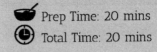 Prep Time: 20 mins

Total Time: 20 mins

Servings per Recipe: 4

Calories	431.6
Fat	32.1g
Cholesterol	47.3mg
Sodium	1044.5mg
Carbohydrates	11.0g
Protein	25.2g

Ingredients

1 lb. eggplant
1 large green bell pepper, chopped
1 garlic clove, crushed
1/2 cup olive oil
1/3 cup red wine vinegar
1 tsp dried oregano, crushed
1 tsp salt

1 (12 1/2 ounce) cans albacore tuna in water, drained
1 large tomatoes, seeded & chopped
1/4 cup feta cheese, crumbled
crisp salad greens

Directions

1. Before you do anything, preheat the oven to 350 F.
2. Slice the eggplants in half and place them on a baking tray.
3. Coat them with olive oil and bake them for 30 min to 45 min until they become soft.
4. Place them aside to cool down for few minutes. Peel them and cut them into dices.
5. Get a mixing bowl: Whisk in it the garlic, oil, vinegar, oregano, and salt.
6. Add the roasted eggplant dices with tomato and tuna and stir them to coat. Refrigerate it for 60 min.
7. Arrange some green leaves on a serving plate. Top it with the eggplant salad.
8. Garnish it with crumbled feta cheese. Serve it.
9. Enjoy.

HANDMADE
Pasta with Sauce

Prep Time: 45 mins
Total Time: 1 hr 45 mins

Servings per Recipe: 8
Calories	811.6
Fat	32.8g
Cholesterol	144.7mg
Sodium	855.1mg
Carbohydrates	79.8g
Protein	46.3g

Ingredients

Pasta
17.5 oz. plain flour
1/2 tsp. salt
water
corn flour, to aid rolling out
1 tbsp. ghee
Sauce
3 1/3 lb. chicken pieces
2 onions, finely chopped
1 garlic clove, minced
1 tbsp. sunflower oil or 1 tbsp. vegetable oil

1 C. of tinned chickpeas
1/4 tsp. black pepper
2 1/4 tsp. ras el hanout spice mix
4 C. water
1 tsp. cinnamon
17.5 oz. long turnips, cut into 6ths
9 oz. potatoes, quartered
9 oz. zucchini, cut into 6ths
1 1/2 tsp. salt

Directions

1. To prepare the pasta:
2. Get a large mixing bowl: Combine in it the flour with salt.
3. Add the water gradually while mixing until you get a soft and smooth dough.
4. Split the dough into 4 pieces. Sprinkle some corn flour on a working surface into a 2 mm thick circle.
5. Repeat the process with the remaining dough pieces then run them through a pasta machine.
6. Place them aside to dry for a few minutes. Adjust the pasta machine to make fine ribbons then run through it the dough sheets.
7. Toss the noodles with some corn flour and place it aside and let it rest for 10 to 12 min.
8. Drizzle over it the melted ghee and toss them to coat.
9. Prepare a steamer. Place in it the noodles and cook it for 8 to 10 min until it done.

10. Place a large skillet over medium heat. Heat in it the oil.
11. Cook in it the chicken with garlic and onion for 10 to 12 min.
12. Stir in the chickpeas with veggies, water, and spices. Cook them for 32 min over low heat with the lid on.
13. Transfer the noodles to a serving plate. Top it with the chicken stew then serve it hot.
14. Enjoy.

CARROT
and Celery Soup

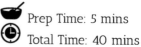 Prep Time: 5 mins
Total Time: 40 mins

Servings per Recipe: 3
Calories	250.0
Fat	1.3g
Cholesterol	0.0mg
Sodium	62.4mg
Carbohydrates	46.6g
Protein	15.5g

Ingredients

1 onion, finely chopped
2 carrots, finely chopped
2 sticks celery, finely chopped
3 garlic cloves, crushed
3 tomatoes, chopped
1/2 tsp. turmeric
1 tsp. ground cumin
1 tsp. ground coriander

5 oz. green lentils
2 pints vegetable stock
1 lemon
1 bunch coriander, chopped

Directions

1. Place a large skillet over medium heat. Heat in it the oil.
2. Cook in it the onion, carrots, and celery for 3 min. Stir in the garlic with tomato, and seasonings.
3. Cook them for 2 to 3 min. Stir in the lentil, stock, salt, and pepper.
4. Put on the lid and lower the heat. Cook them for 35 min.
5. Once the time is up, stir in the coriander with lemon juice. Serve it hot.
6. Enjoy.

Dolmas
Biskra

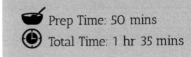
Prep Time: 50 mins
Total Time: 1 hr 35 mins

Servings per Recipe: 1

Calories	30.0
Fat	0.5g
Cholesterol	0.0mg
Sodium	138.5mg
Carbohydrates	5.7g
Protein	0.7g

Ingredients

Insides
50 grape leaves
1 large red pepper, diced
1 large red vine-ripened tomatoes, diced
1/2 large onion, diced
4 garlic cloves, minced
1 1/2 C. basmati rice or 1 1/2 C. long grain rice
1 tsp. paprika
1/2 tsp. cinnamon
1/2 tsp. ras el hanout spice mix
1 tbsp. olive oil
4 tbsp. water
salt and black pepper

Sauce
1/2 large onion, diced
1 large vine-ripened tomatoes, diced
2 garlic cloves, minced
1/2 tsp. cinnamon
1 chicken stock cube
4 C. water
1 tsp. lemons or 1 tsp. lime juice
salt and black pepper

Directions

1. To prepare the leaves:
2. Bring a large salted pot of water to a boil.
3. Trim and wash the leaves then cook them in the hot water for 16 min.
4. Drain them and place them aside.
5. To prepare the filling:
6. Place a large pan over medium heat. Heat in it some olive oil.
7. Add to it the peppers with tomato and onion. Cook them for 3 min.
8. Stir in the garlic and cook them for 3 to 4 min. Stir in the spices and cook them for 1 min.
9. Once the time is up, turn off the heat and add the water with remaining olive oil and rice.

10. Place the filling aside to cool down.

11. To prepare the broth:

12. Place a large pot over medium heat. Heat in it the olive oil. Cook in it the tomato with onion for 3 min.

13. Stir in the spices with the stock cube, water, and lemon juice. Cook them for 16 min.

14. Once the time is up, turn off the heat and strain the broth.

15. Place a leaf on a plate. Put in it 1 tsp. of the filling.

16. Pull the sides over the filling then roll it forward like a cigar.

17. Repeat the process with the remaining ingredients.

18. Arrange the stuffed leaves in a pot then place on top of them a plate.

19. Pour the hot broth on top then put on the lid. Let them cook for 26 min over low heat.

20. Serve your stuffed leaves hot.

21. Enjoy.

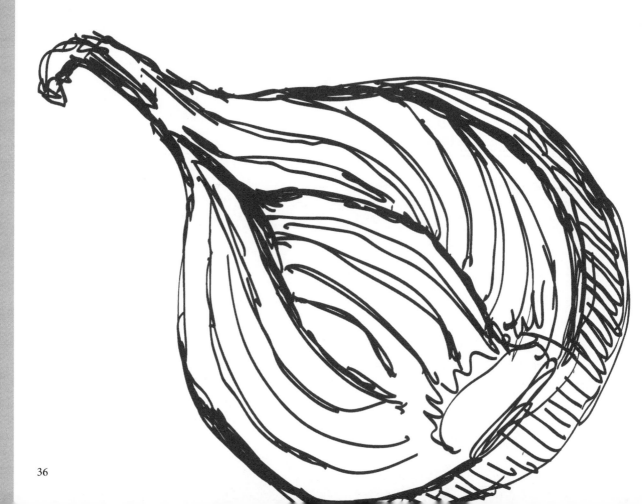

African
Tuna Sandwiches with Handmade Bread

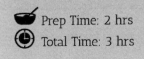 Prep Time: 2 hrs

Total Time: 3 hrs

Servings per Recipe: 4

Calories	948.8
Fat	30.5g
Cholesterol	196.5mg
Sodium	1516.7mg
Carbohydrates	138.6g
Protein	31.4g

Ingredients

Sauce
500 g pumpkin
4 garlic cloves, mashed
1/4 tsp cayenne pepper
1/4 tsp paprika
1/4 cup oil
1 tsp caraway seed, ground
1 lemon, juice
Buns
4 cups flour
2 tsps yeast

2 tbsps oil
1 tsp salt
1 egg
1 1/4 cups water
Filling
3 potatoes, boiled cubed
4 eggs, hardboiled, sliced
4 pickles, sliced lengthwise
3.5 oz. olives, pitted
3.5 oz. canned tuna, drained

Directions

1. To prepare the pumpkin sauce:
2. Place a pan over medium heat. Heat in it the oil. Stir in it the garlic with pumpkin for 7 min.
3. Stir in the cayenne pepper with caraway seeds, 1 cup of water, a pinch of salt and lemon juice. Cook them until they become soft.
4. Mash them until they become smooth. Place it aside.
5. To prepare the buns:
6. Get a mixing bowl: Mix in it all the dough ingredients until you get a smooth dough.
7. Transfer it to a floured surface and knead it for 5 min. Divide it into 20 balls.
8. Place them on greased baking trays then cover them with a kitchen towel. Let them rest for 45 min.
9. Place a deep pan over medium heat. Heat in it 2 inches of oil. Deep fry in it the dough ball until they become golden brown.

10. Drain the bread rolls and place them on paper towels to drain.

11. To prepare the filling:

12. Get a mixing bowl: Stir in it the eggs with pickles, olives, tuna, potatoes, a pinch of salt and pepper.

13. Slice the bread rolls in half. Spread the pumpkin sauce in the bottom halves. Top them with the tuna mixture.

14. Cover them with the top halves. Serve your sandwiches immediately.

15. Enjoy.

Chili Sausage and Potato Stew

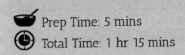

Prep Time: 5 mins
Total Time: 1 hr 15 mins

Servings per Recipe: 4
Calories	374.9
Fat	17.8g
Cholesterol	279.0mg
Sodium	152.7mg
Carbohydrates	40.5g
Protein	14.4g

Ingredients

3 - 4 tbsps olive oil
4 medium potatoes, cubed
1 - 2 tbsp tomato paste
1 - 4 tsp harissa
3 - 4 garlic cloves, skinned and crushed
2 - 3 dried chilies, seeded and chopped
2 tsps crushed caraway seeds

2 tsps paprika
6 small spicy sausage, sliced
6 eggs
salt

Directions

1. Place skillet over medium heat. Heat in it the oil.
2. Cook in it the potatoes for 3 min. Stir in the tomato paste with harissa, garlic, caraway seeds and paprika.
3. Season them with a pinch of salt. Add enough water to cover the potatoes.
4. Put on the lid and let them cook for 45 min over low heat. Stir in the sausages and let them cook for 16 min.
5. Get a mixing bowl: Whisk in it the eggs with a pinch of salt and pepper.
6. Add it to the stew and mix them well. Let them cook until the eggs are done.
7. Adjust the seasoning of your stew then serve it warm with some bread.
8. Enjoy.

ALGERIAN
Lamb Shoulder

Prep Time: 20 mins
Total Time: 1 hr 40 mins

Servings per Recipe: 4
Calories   787.1
Fat   59.5g
Cholesterol   163.3mg
Sodium   744.0mg
Carbohydrates   22.1g
Protein   42.3g

Ingredients

3 tbsp oil
2 lbs boneless lamb shoulder, 1-inch chunks
1 medium onion, chopped
4 garlic cloves, minced
1 tsp. salt
1/4 tsp. fresh ground black pepper
1 tsp. ground cumin
1/2 tsp. cayenne pepper
1/2 tsp. saffron or 1/2 tsp. turmeric

4 C. water
1 1/2 lbs green beans, 2-inch pieces
2 tomatoes, diced
1 medium onion, sliced in rings
4 tbsp parsley, chopped
1 tsp. ground cumin

Directions

1. Place a pot over medium heat. Heat in it the oil.
2. Cook in it the lamb with garlic and onion for 5 min.
3. Stir in the salt, pepper, 1 tsp. cumin, cayenne, and saffron. Cook them for 2 min.
4. Stir in the tomato with water. Heat them until they start boiling. Lower the heat and put on the lid.
5. Cook them for 46 min. Stir in the green beans and cook them for 10 to 12 min.
6. Sir in the onion with parsley and 1 tsp. of cumin. Cook them for an extra 10 to 12 min.
7. Adjust the seasoning of your stew then serve it hot with some couscous.
8. Enjoy.

Lamb
Tagine with Saffron

🥣 Prep Time: 20 mins

🕐 Total Time: 3 hrs 20 mins

Servings per Recipe: 4

Calories	933.8
Fat	40.6g
Cholesterol	120.0mg
Sodium	923.9mg
Carbohydrates	89.4g
Protein	62.1g

Ingredients

2 lbs. lamb, cut into pieces
3 lbs. artichokes
3 lbs. green peas
1 tsp ginger
1 pinch saffron
1 clove garlic
3 tbsps olive oil

1 preserved lemon
1/2 lb. olive, green
1 bunch parsley
lemon juice

Directions

1. Get a large mixing bowl: Mix in it the olive oil with garlic, ginger, and saffron.
2. Add the lamb pieces and toss them to coat.
3. Place a tagine or stew pot over medium heat. Heat in it 1 tbsp of olive oil.
4. Brown in it the meat pieces for 3 to 4 min on each side.
5. Arrange the artichoke hearts on top followed by the olives, preserved lemon, 1/2 cup of water, a pinch of salt and pepper.
6. Put on the lid and let it cook over the lowest heat setting for 1 h 30 min to 2 h until the meat is done.
7. Serve your lamb tagine warm with some bread.
8. Enjoy.

ARABIAN
Meatball Soup

Prep Time: 20 mins
Total Time: 2 hrs 5 mins

Servings per Recipe: 6
Calories	707.9
Fat	55.9g
Cholesterol	140.6mg
Sodium	1959.0mg
Carbohydrates	18.0g
Protein	33.0g

Ingredients

Meat
2 tbsps olive oil
1 small yellow onion, minced
1 lb. ground chuck
1 tbsp ground cumin
1 tbsp ground black pepper
1 tbsp cilantro, minced
1 tbsp parsley, minced
2 1/4 tsps kosher salt
1 1/2 tsps paprika
3/4 tsp ground cinnamon
1 egg, beaten

Stew
1/4 cup olive oil
1 lb. beef short rib
kosher salt & ground black pepper
4 garlic cloves, chopped
1 large yellow onion, minced
5 cups beef stock
6 ounces spinach leaves, chopped
1 (16 ounces) cans white kidney beans,
rinsed drained
cooked couscous

Directions

1. To prepare the meatballs:
2. Place a soup pot over high heat. Heat in it 1 tbsp of oil.
3. Cook in it the onion for 6 min. Transfer it to a mixing bowl with the chuck, cumin, pepper, cilantro, parsley, salt, paprika, cinnamon, and egg. Shape the mixture into meatballs.
4. Heat another tbsp of oil in the saucepan. Brown in it the meatballs for 5 min. Drain them and place them aside.
5. To prepare the soup:
6. Sprinkle some salt and pepper all over the ribs. Brown them for 7 min. Drain them and place them aside.
7. Stir the onion with garlic into the saucepan. Let them cook for 6 min.
8. Add the ribs back with stock. Cook them until they start boiling. Lower the heat and let them cook for 60 min.

9. Stir in the meatballs and let them cook for an extra 9 min. Stir in the beans with spinach for 5 min.

10. Adjust the seasoning of your ribs and meatballs stew. Serve it hot. Enjoy.

WHOLE CHICKEN
Mediterranean Style

Prep Time: 15 mins
Total Time: 55 mins

Servings per Recipe: 4
Calories	356.3
Fat	23.4g
Cholesterol	100.3mg
Sodium	1393.7mg
Carbohydrates	13.3g
Protein	24.0g

Ingredients

1 chicken, cut-up
2 tsp. salt
1/4 tsp. pepper
2 tbsp. butter
1/2 C. chicken broth
1 garlic clove, crushed
1 medium eggplant, pared and diced

1 medium onion, chopped
2 fresh tomatoes, peeled and chopped
1/4 tsp. thyme
1 tbsp. parsley, minced

Directions

1. Coat the chicken with paprika, 1 tsp. of salt and pepper.
2. Place a large pan over medium heat. Heat in it the butter until it melts.
3. Cook in it the chicken pieces for 3 to 4 min on each side. Drain them and place them aside.
4. Pour the broth into the pan. Stir in the garlic, eggplant, onion, and tomatoes; sprinkle with remaining salt, thyme, and parsley.
5. Heat them until they start boiling. Stir in the chicken and put on the lid.
6. Cook them for 32 min over low heat until it the chicken done. Serve it warm.
7. Enjoy.

Mint
and Tomato Lentils with Lamb

Prep Time: 15 mins
Total Time: 1 hr 5 mins

Servings per Recipe: 4
Calories	368.4
Fat	1.1g
Cholesterol	0.0mg
Sodium	185.0mg
Carbohydrates	64.4g
Protein	25.9g

Ingredients

2 C. green lentils, soaked overnight and drained
1 onion, finely chopped
3 garlic cloves, minced
1 carrot, grated
1 courgette, grated
1 tsp. dried mint
1 tsp. ras el hanout, see appendix
olive oil, to fry

2 pints water
1 lamb stock cube or 1 beef stock cube
salt & pepper
4 pieces lamb or 4 pieces chicken
1/2 tsp. tomato puree

Directions

1. Place a pan over medium heat. Heat in it a splash of oil.
2. Cook in it the garlic with onion for 4 min. Stir in the meat and cook them for another 4 min.
3. Transfer the mixture to a pressure cooker. Stir in the remaining ingredients.
4. Put on the lid and cook them for 40 to 46 min on high pressure.
5. Adjust the seasoning of your stew then serve it hot.
6. Enjoy.

GARLICKY
Lamb

 Prep Time: 15 mins

Total Time: 50 mins

Servings per Recipe: 4
Calories	382.7
Fat	17.2g
Cholesterol	741.9mg
Sodium	427.9mg
Carbohydrates	13.8g
Protein	42.3g

Ingredients

28 oz. fresh lamb liver, 1 inch wide
pieces
6-8 garlic cloves, minced
2 C. chopped tinned tomatoes with juice
1/2 C. chopped fresh coriander
2-3 tsp. fresh ground cumin
salt & freshly ground black pepper

1 C. water
2 tbsp. good quality olive oil

Directions

1. Place a large pan over medium heat. Heat in it the oil.
2. Cook in it the liver pieces for 2 to 3 min on each side.
3. Lower the heat and let them cook for an extra 6 min. Stir in the garlic with cumin.
4. Cook them for 1 min while stirring. Stir in the tomato with a pinch of salt and pepper.
5. Cook them for 2 min. Stir in the water and put on the lid. Cook them for 26 min.
6. Once the time is up, add the coriander.
7. Adjust the seasoning of your liver stew then serve it hot with some rice.
8. Enjoy.

Fathia's
Bean Bowls

🥣 Prep Time: 15 mins
🕐 Total Time: 2 hrs 30 mins

Servings per Recipe: 4
Calories	832.3
Fat	43.3g
Cholesterol	187.2mg
Sodium	366.6mg
Carbohydrates	46.6g
Protein	63.3g

Ingredients

1 C. dried lima beans, soaked overnight and drained
2 tbsp. olive oil
26.5 oz. lamb
2 medium brown onions, coarsely chopped
2 garlic cloves, crushed
2 medium carrots, coarsely chopped
2 celery ribs, trimmed and coarsely chopped

2 C. chicken stock
4 C. water
14 oz. chopped tomatoes
4 tbsp. chopped fresh coriander
2 tbsp. lemon juice

Directions

1. Place a pot over medium heat. Heat in it the oil.
2. Cook in it the lamb pieces for 2 min on each side.
3. Stir in the veggies and cook them for 4 min. Stir in the stock with water and beans.
4. Heat them until they start boiling. Lower the heat and put on the lid.
5. Cook them for 60 min while discarding the rising foam on top every 30 min.
6. Once the time is up, drain the lamb pieces and shred them.
7. Stir them back into the pot with tomatoes. Put on the lid and cook them for an extra 60 min.
8. Turn off the heat and add the lemon juice with coriander.
9. Adjust the seasoning of your soup then serve it hot.
10. Enjoy.

ALGERIAN
Mash for Toast

Prep Time: 10 mins
Total Time: 30 mins

Servings per Recipe: 6
Calories   43.0
Fat   0.4g
Cholesterol   0.0mg
Sodium   4.3mg
Carbohydrates   10.0g
Protein   1.7g

Ingredients

2 eggplants,1/2 inch slices
2 garlic cloves, crushed
1 tsp. sweet paprika
1 1/2 tsp. cumin, ground

1/2 tsp. sugar
1 tbsp. lemon juice

Directions

1. Season the eggplant slices with some salt. Place them in a sieve and let them sit for 32 min.
2. Once the time is up, rinse them and dry them.
3. Place a large skillet over medium heat. Heat in it 1/4 inch of oil.
4. Cook in it the eggplant slices until they become golden brown.
5. Drain them and place them on some paper towels to cool down for few minutes.
6. Finely chop them and place them in a sieve to drain for 5 min.
7. Get a large mixing bowl: Combine in it the chopped eggplant with cumin, sugar, and paprika.
8. Stir them to coat. Pour the mixture into a hot pan and cook them for 2 to 3 min.
9. Stir in the lemon juice with a pinch of salt then serve it hot.
10. Enjoy.

North African Frittatas

🍲 Prep Time: 15 mins

🕐 Total Time: 1 hr 25 mins

Servings per Recipe: 4

Calories	230.6
Fat	15.0g
Cholesterol	268.8mg
Sodium	360.9mg
Carbohydrates	8.8g
Protein	15.5g

Ingredients

1 eggplant
1 tbsp extra virgin olive oil
1 medium onion, chopped
1 medium red bell pepper, diced
8 large eggs
1/2 bunch flat leaf parsley, minced
2 garlic cloves, minced
1/4 tsp rose water
1/2 tsp salt
1/4 tsp ground pepper

1/8 tsp ground cinnamon
1 tsp harissa, dissolved in 1 tbsp of water, see appendix
1/4 lb. gruyere cheese, grated

Directions

1. Before you do anything, preheat the oven to 450 F.
2. Use a sharp knife to make slits in the eggplant without cutting it all the way through.
3. Place it on a baking sheet and coat it with olive oil.
4. Roast it in the oven for 22 min. Decrease the oven temperature to 350 min.
5. Place the eggplant aside to lose heat for 10 min. Peel it and dice it.
6. Place a pan over medium heat. Heat in it 1 tbsp of olive oil.
7. Cook in it the bell pepper with onion for 9 min. Stir in the garlic with eggplant, and a pinch of salt.
8. Cook them for an extra 2 min. parsley, rose water, salt, pepper, cinnamon, and harissa.
9. Fold the eggplant mixture into the eggs with cheese. Pour the mixture in a greased baking pan.
10. Cook it in the oven for 32 min. Allow your omelet to rest for 12 min then serve it.
11. Enjoy.

SEMOLINA BREAD
with Chili Spread

Prep Time: 20 mins
Total Time: 40 mins

Servings per Recipe: 6
Calories	799.2
Fat	26.6g
Cholesterol	0.0mg
Sodium	591.8mg
Carbohydrates	118.2g
Protein	20.7g

Ingredients

Bread
2 lbs. semolina, medium ground
1 1/2 tsp. salt
3 C. water
4 tbsp. olive oil
6 tbsp. olive oil, for frying
Spread/Dip
2 large red bell peppers

4 vine ripened tomatoes
1 tbsp. olive oil
5 garlic cloves, minced
1 green chili pepper
salt

Directions

1. To prepare the pepper dip/spread:
2. Before you do anything, preheat the oven broiler.
3. Place the bell peppers with tomatoes on a baking sheet.
4. Broil them in the oven for 8 min while flipping them every 2 to 3 min.
5. Allow them to cool down completely then peel them and discard the seeds.
6. Place a large skillet. Heat in it 1 tbsp. of olive oil. Cook in it the garlic with chili for 1 min.
7. Drain them and transfer them to a food processor. Add to them the roasted tomatoes and bell peppers. Pulse them several times until they become finely chopped.
8. Pour the mixture into a bowl and place it in the fridge until ready to serve.
9. To prepare the bread:
10. Get a large mixing bowl: Mix in it the semolina with 4 tbsp. of olive oil and salt.
11. Add the water gradually while mixing until you get smooth elastic dough.
12. Shape it into 6 balls then roll them until they become 1/4 inch thick.
13. Place a large pan over medium heat. Heat in it 1 tbsp. of olive oil.
14. Cook in it the dough circles for 3 to 5 min on each side until they become golden brown.
15. Enjoy.

Grilled
Salad

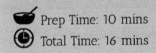 Prep Time: 10 mins

Total Time: 16 mins

Servings per Recipe: 4

Calories	126.5
Fat	8.4 g
Cholesterol	2.2 mg
Sodium	72.4 mg
Carbohydrates	11.0 g
Protein	4.9 g

Ingredients

2 tbsp extra virgin olive oil
1 tbsp lemon juice
1 small garlic clove, minced
1/2 tsp Dijon mustard
1/8 tsp Worcestershire sauce
1/4 tsp black pepper

2 tbsp grated parmesan cheese
olive oil flavored cooking spray
2 romaine lettuce hearts

Directions

1. Get a mixing bowl: Mix in it the oil, lemon juice, garlic, mustard, Worcestershire, and pepper.
2. Add the parmesan cheese and combine them well to make the dressing.
3. Place it in the fridge until ready to serve.
4. Before you do anything, preheat the grill and grease it.
5. Slice the romaine hearts in half lengthwise. Coat them with a cooking spray.
6. Grill them for 3 to 4 min on each side. Serve them warm with the cheese dressing.
7. Enjoy.

MENDOZA
Kabobs

Prep Time: 30 mins
Total Time: 45 mins

Servings per Recipe: 4
Calories   532.5
Fat   40.9 g
Cholesterol   92.8 mg
Sodium   96.2 mg
Carbohydrates   9.7 g
Protein   31.5 g

Ingredients

4 chicken breasts, diced
1/2 red bell pepper, cut into squares
1/2 green bell pepper, cut into squares
2 yellow onions, cut into eighths
1 C. cherry tomatoes
bamboo skewer
1/2 C. oil

3 cloves garlic, chopped
1 tsp paprika
1/2 tsp Mexican oregano
kosher salt
black peppercorns

Directions

1. Before you do anything, preheat the grill and grease it.
2. Get a food processor: Combine in it the Oil, Garlic, Paprika, Oregano, Salt, and Peppercorns.
3. Process them several times until they become smooth to make the marinade.
4. Get a large mixing bowl: Combine in it the chicken dices with marinade.
5. Cover the bowl and let it sit for at least 20 min.
6. Before you do anything else, preheat the grill and grease it.
7. Thread the chicken dices with onion, peppers, and cherry tomatoes onto skewers while alternating between them.
8. Grill them for 8 to 10 min on each side. Serve them warm.
9. Enjoy.

Grilled
Gazebo Salad

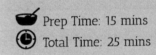 Prep Time: 15 mins

Total Time: 25 mins

Servings per Recipe: 8

Calories	336.1
Fat	18.2 g
Cholesterol	29.5 mg
Sodium	428.5 mg
Carbohydrates	32.6 g
Protein	10.7 g

Ingredients

Vegetables
4 cloves roasted garlic, minced
1 red pepper, quartered
1 portabella mushroom
1 onion, sliced
1 zucchini, sliced into 4 long strips
3 tbsp olive oil
3 tbsp balsamic vinegar
tsp Italian seasoning
Dressing
2 cloves garlic, minced
1/4 C. olive oil

1/8 C. balsamic vinegar
1 sprig rosemary, stem discarded leaves chopped
Salad
16 oz. cheese tortellini
1/2 C. provolone cheese, diced
4 oz. black olives
salt and pepper

Directions

1. Get a large zip lock bag: Combine in it the veggies with oil, vinegar, and Italian seasoning.
2. Seal the bag and let them sit for 60 min in the fridge.
3. Before you do anything, preheat the grill and grease it.
4. Grill the veggies for 3 to 4 min on each side.
5. Place them aside to cool down for a bit. Dice them.
6. Get a food processor: Combine in it the salad dressing ingredients. Blend them smooth.
7. Get a large mixing bowl: Combine in it the grilled veggies with tortellini, cheese, olives, dressing, a pinch of salt and pepper.
8. Stir them to coat. Adjust the seasoning of your salad then serve it with extra toppings of your choice.
9. Enjoy.

SOUTHWEST
Rib-Eye Steaks

Prep Time: 2 hrs 10 mins
Total Time: 2 hrs 15 mins

Servings per Recipe: 9

Calories	379.4
Fat	37.4 g
Cholesterol	0.0 mg
Sodium	1191.8 mg
Carbohydrates	11.8 g
Protein	2.7 g

Ingredients

4 oz. bunch flat leaf parsley, stemmed, chopped
4 oz. bunch cilantro, chopped
3 garlic cloves, minced
2 tbsp ground cumin
1 tbsp ground coriander
2 tbsp sweet paprika
1 tsp smoked paprika
1 tsp cayenne pepper
1 pinch saffron thread

1/4 C. lemon juice
1 C. olive oil
1 tbsp kosher salt
6 boneless rib-eye steaks, excess fat trimmed, cubed
2 red onions, chopped
2 red bell peppers, chopped

Directions

1. Get a blender: Place in it the parsley with cilantro, garlic, cumin, coriander, paprika, cayenne, and saffron.
2. Process them until them until they become smooth.
3. Combine in the olive oil with lemon juice and salt. Blend them smooth to make the marinade.
4. Get a mixing bowl: Stir in it the steak cubes with half of the marinade.
5. Cover the bowl and let it sit in the fridge for 120 min.
6. Before you do anything, preheat the grill and grease it.
7. Thread the steak cubes with onion and peppers onto skewers while alternating between them.
8. Grill them for 7 to 8 min on each side.
9. Serve your steak skewers warm with the remaining marinade.
10. Enjoy.

A Whole
Chicken in Belize

🥣 Prep Time: 10 mins

🕐 Total Time: 45 mins

Servings per Recipe: 4

Calories	779.1
Fat	56.7 g
Cholesterol	243.8 mg
Sodium	1569.3 mg
Carbohydrates	4.0 g
Protein	60.3 g

Ingredients

1/3 C. soy sauce
2 tbsp lime juice
5 garlic cloves
2 tsp ground cumin
1 tsp paprika
1/2 tsp dried oregano

1 tbsp vegetable oil
1 whole chicken, quartered

Directions

1. Get a food processor: Combine in it the soy sauce, lime juice, garlic, cumin, paprika, oregano, 1/2 tsp pepper, and oil.

2. Get a large zip lock bag: place in it the chicken pieces. Pour over it the marinade.

3. Seal the bag and let it sit in the fridge for 7 h to 26 h.

4. Before you do anything, preheat the grill and grease it.

5. Grill the chicken pieces for 15 to 18 min on each side. Serve them warm.

6. Enjoy.

TOPPED
Seafood Tacos

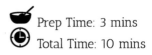 Prep Time: 3 mins
Total Time: 10 mins

Servings per Recipe: 2
Calories	316.4
Fat	18.8 g
Cholesterol	7.2 mg
Sodium	152.2 mg
Carbohydrates	32.3 g
Protein	8.3 g

Ingredients

Sauce
1 large avocado, chopped
1/2 C. water
1/4 C. loosely packed cilantro
1/2-1 large pickled jalapeno pepper, seeded
1 tbsp fresh limes
1 large garlic clove
kosher salt
black pepper
Marinade
1 tbsp olive oil
1/2 limes, zest

1 tbsp limes
1 garlic clove, minced
kosher salt
pepper
Tacos
4 -6 large sea scallops
olive oil
1/2 C. green cabbage, sliced
1/4 C. red onion, sliced
1 -1 1/2 tbsp cilantro, chopped
4 corn tortillas

Directions

1. Get a food processor: Combine it all the sauce ingredients. Blend them smooth to make the sauce. Get a mixing bowl: Whisk in it the marinade ingredients. Cut each scallop in half. Stir into it into the marinade.

2. Put on the lid and chill it in the fridge for 16 min. Get a mixing bowl: Combine in it the cabbage with onion and cilantro.

3. Place a large pan over medium heat. Hat in it the olive oil.

4. Drain the scallops from the marinade. Cook them in the hot oil for 40 sec to 1 min on each side.

5. Heat the tortillas in a pan or a microwave. Place them on serving plates. Top each one of them with the cabbage salad, scallops, and avocado sauce. Wrap your tortillas then toast them in a grill pan or a grill. Serve them warm.

6. Enjoy.

Garlicky
Fish Griller

Prep Time: 5 mins
Total Time: 20 mins

Servings per Recipe: 4
Calories	261.3
Fat	28.7 g
Cholesterol	0.0 mg
Sodium	146.3 mg
Carbohydrates	2.4 g
Protein	0.1 g

Ingredients

4 fish steaks
1/2 tbsp olive oil
lemon juice
1 tbsp Greek oregano, chopped
salt
Dressing

2 lemons, juice
1/2 C. extra-virgin olive oil
1 pinch sea salt
1 garlic clove

Directions

1. Before you do anything, preheat the grill and grease it.
2. Coat the fish steaks with olive oil and lemon juice.
3. Season them with oregano, a pinch of salt and pepper.
4. Grill them for 5 to 7 min on each side.
5. Get a blender: Combine in it the dressing ingredients. Blend them smooth.
6. Drizzle the dressing over the fish steaks then serve them.
7. Enjoy.

HONEY
Basil Chicken

Prep Time: 6 mins
Total Time: 22 mins

Servings per Recipe: 4
Calories	247.4
Fat	5.7 g
Cholesterol	108.9 mg
Sodium	267.3 mg
Carbohydrates	9.6 g
Protein	37.6 g

Ingredients

3 tbsp balsamic vinegar
1 tbsp Dijon mustard
1 tbsp honey
2 garlic cloves, minced
1 1/2 lbs. boneless skinless chicken breasts

1 C. basil leaf, chopped
4 C. baby arugula, chopped
1/4 C. sun-dried tomato packed in oil, chopped

Directions

1. To prepare the marinade:
2. Place a heavy saucepan over medium heat. Combine in it the vinegar, mustard, honey, garlic, pepper, and oil.
3. Heat it until it starts boiling. Lower the heat and let it simmer for 4 to 6 min. Before you do anything, preheat the grill and grease it.
4. Place the chicken breasts between 2 pieces of a plastic wrap.
5. Use a meat tenderizer to flatten them until they become 1/2 inch thick. Season the chicken breasts with a pinch of salt and pepper.
6. Grill them for 4 to 6 min on each side. Place them aside and let rest for 5 min. Cut them into strips.
7. Get a large mixing bowl: Combine in it the chicken strips with the heated marinade.
8. Stir them to coat and season them with a pinch of salt and pepper.
9. Arrange the basil with arugula and sun-dried tomatoes on a serving plate.
10. Layover them the chicken mixture. Serve them immediately.
11. Enjoy.

Hot
Jamaican Filets

Prep Time: 1 hr 5 mins

Total Time: 1 hr 11 mins

Servings per Recipe: 4
Calories	258.0
Fat	8.3 g
Cholesterol	99.0 mg
Sodium	142.1 mg
Carbohydrates	2.2 g
Protein	41.4 g

Ingredients

2 tbsp olive oil
2 garlic cloves , minced
1 1/2 tbsp lime juice
1 tbsp fresh ginger , minced
1 scotch bonnet pepper , seeded and sliced

4 fish fillets
salt
black pepper

Directions

1. Get a mixing bowl: Whisk in it the oil, garlic, lime juice, ginger, and scotch bonnet.
2. Add the fish fillets and stir them to coat. Cover the bowl and let it sit for 60 min in the fridge.
3. Before you do anything, preheat the grill and grease it.
4. Drain the fish fillets. Sprinkle over them some salt and pepper.
5. Grill them for 3 to 5 min on each side. Serve them warm.
6. Enjoy.

SOUTHWEST
Sirloin

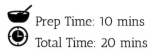

Prep Time: 10 mins
Total Time: 20 mins

Servings per Recipe: 4
Calories	180.1
Fat	5.5 g
Cholesterol	68.0 mg
Sodium	453.9 mg
Carbohydrates	6.6 g
Protein	26.1 g

Ingredients

3 tbsp chili powder
2 tsp brown sugar
2 tsp pepper
2 garlic cloves, minced
1/2 tsp salt
1/2 tsp dried oregano

1/4 tsp ground cumin
1 lb. boneless beef top sirloin steak
salsa

Directions

1. Get a mixing bowl: Mix in it the chili powder, brown sugar, pepper, garlic, salt, oregano, and cumin.
2. Massage the mixture into the steak and let it sit for at least 30 min.
3. Before you do anything, preheat the grill and grease it.
4. Grill it for 6 to 8 min on each side. Serve it warm with some salsa.
5. Enjoy.

Blackened
Chicken Cutlets

Prep Time: 5 mins
Total Time: 13 mins

Servings per Recipe: 4
Calories	154.2
Fat	1.7 g
Cholesterol	68.4 mg
Sodium	1836.4 mg
Carbohydrates	5.3 g
Protein	28.2 g

Ingredients

4 -6 boneless skinless chicken breast
halves
Spice Mix
4 tsp granulated onion
4 tsp granulated garlic
1 tbsp kosher salt

2 tsp chili powder
2 tsp ground black pepper
extra virgin olive oil

Directions

1. Before you do anything, preheat the grill and grease it.
2. Get a mixing bowl: Combine in it the onion with garlic, salt, chili powder and black pepper.
3. Coat the chicken dices with the spice mixture. Thread them onto skewers.
4. Grill them for 10 to 14 min. Serve them warm.
5. Enjoy.

GRILLED
Bread

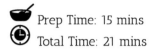 Prep Time: 15 mins

Total Time: 21 mins

Servings per Recipe: 4
Calories	112.1
Fat	11.5 g
Cholesterol	30.5 mg
Sodium	84.0 mg
Carbohydrates	2.3 g
Protein	0.6 g

Ingredients

1/4 C. butter
2 tbsp chopped shallots
1/2 tsp chopped garlic
4 slices round sourdough loaf
1/4 C. torn basil leaf

2 medium Roma tomatoes, cut into 6 slices
2 tsp red wine vinegar

Directions

1. Before you do anything, preheat the grill and grease it.
2. Place a heavy saucepan over medium heat. Heat in it the butter.
3. Cook in it the garlic with shallots for 2 min.
4. Toast the bread slices on the grill for 1 to 2 min on each side.
5. Coat one side of them with butter.
6. Place the buttered side facing down followed by tomato slices and vinegar.
7. Serve them warm.
8. Enjoy.

Fish
Africano

Prep Time: 15 mins
Total Time: 45 mins

Servings per Recipe: 4
Calories	186.9
Fat	7.6 g
Cholesterol	59.4 mg
Sodium	238.3 mg
Carbohydrates	6.4 g
Protein	24.3 g

Ingredients

1/4 C. nonfat plain yogurt
1/4 C. chopped parsley
1/4 C. chopped cilantro
2 tbsp lemon juice
1 tbsp extra virgin olive oil
3 garlic cloves, minced
1 1/2 tsp paprika
1 tsp ground cumin
1/4 tsp salt

1/8 tsp ground pepper
1 lb. center-cut salmon fillet, cut into 4 portions
1 lemon, cut into wedges

Directions

1. Get a mixing bowl: Whisk in it the yogurt, parsley, cilantro, lemon juice, oil, garlic, paprika, cumin, salt, and pepper.
2. Reserve 1/4 C. of dressing in the fridge until ready to serve.
3. Get a zip lock bag: Combine in it the fish fillets with the remaining dressing.
4. Seal the bag and shake it to coat. Chill it in the fridge to marinade for 35 min.
5. Before you do anything, preheat the grill and grease it.
6. Drain the salmon fillets and grill them for 5 to 7 min on each side.
7. Serve them warm with the reserved dressing sauce.
8. Enjoy.

HOW TO
Braise Brussel Sprouts

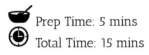 Prep Time: 5 mins
Total Time: 15 mins

Servings per Recipe: 4
Calories	163.5
Fat	14.0g
Cholesterol	0.0mg
Sodium	24.4mg
Carbohydrates	8.8g
Protein	3.0g

Ingredients

1 lb. Brussels sprout
4 - 6 tbsp extra - virgin olive oil
3 - 4 garlic cloves, minced
lemon juice
salt

white pepper

Directions

1. Discard the brown leaves of the brussels sprouts. Slice them in half.
2. Place a heavy saucepan over medium heat. Heat in it the oil.
3. Cook in it the brussels sprouts for 8 to 10 min until they become golden brown while stirring.
4. Stir in the garlic and cook them for one minute.
5. Add the lemon juice with a pinch of salt and pepper. Toss them to coat and serve them warm.
6. Enjoy.

Red Bell Brussel Sprouts

🍲 Prep Time: 20 mins
🕐 Total Time: 40 mins

Servings per Recipe: 6

Calories	187.6
Fat	12.1g
Cholesterol	30.5mg
Sodium	121.1mg
Carbohydrates	18.5g
Protein	5.8g

Ingredients

2 lbs. Brussels sprouts, trimmed
2 red bell peppers, seeded, sliced
1 onions, sliced
2 garlic cloves, minced
6 tbsp butter
salt

pepper
2 tbsp lemon juice

Directions

1. Use a sharp knife to make a cut in the shape of X in the bottom of each brussels sprout.
2. Place a large skillet over medium heat. Heat in it the butter.
3. Cook in it the garlic with pepper and onion for 4 min.
4. Stir in the brussels sprouts with a pinch of salt and pepper. Cook them for 4 to 6 min.
5. Stir in the lemon rind then serve them warm.
6. Enjoy.

LOVER'S
Brussel Sprouts

Prep Time: 10 mins
Total Time: 25 mins

Servings per Recipe: 2

Calories	229.2
Fat	19.5g
Cholesterol	22.9mg
Sodium	110.0mg
Carbohydrates	12.6g
Protein	4.3g

Ingredients

15 Brussels sprouts halved lengthwise
1 1/2 tbsp butter
1 1/2 tbsp olive oil
3 cloves garlic, smashed with the flat of
a knife

grated parmesan cheese
salt and pepper

Directions

1. Place a large pan over medium heat. Heat in the oil with butter.

2. Lower the heat and add the garlic. Fry it for 1 to 2 min until it becomes brown.

3. Drain it and discard it. Stir in the brussels sprouts and cook them for 12 to 16 min until they become soft.

4. Season them with a pinch of salt and pepper. Garnish them with parmesan cheese then serve them warm.

5. Enjoy.

Thai Style
Brussel Sprouts

Prep Time: 10 mins
Total Time: 25 mins

Servings per Recipe: 3
Calories   185.0
Fat   14.3g
Cholesterol   0.0mg
Sodium   730.9mg
Carbohydrates   12.0g
Protein   5.3g

Ingredients

1 lb. Brussels sprout, trimmed and halved
3 tbsp olive oil
2 tbsp low sodium soy sauce
1 tbsp sriracha sauce
1 1/2 tsp Dijon mustard
1/2 tsp ground ginger

1 tsp chopped garlic
sesame seeds

Directions

1. Get a mixing bowl: Whisk in it the olive oil, soy sauce, Sriracha, mustard, ginger, and garlic powder.
2. Add the brussels sprouts and toss them to coat. Let them sit for 5 to 7 min.
3. Place a large pot over high heat.
4. Add to it the brussels sprouts mixture and cook them for 10 to 14 min while occasionally stirring.
5. Garnish them with sesame seeds then serve them warm.
6. Enjoy.

BRUSSEL SPROUTS
with Cannellini

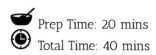 Prep Time: 20 mins

Total Time: 40 mins

Servings per Recipe: 8	
Calories	254.4
Fat	17.2g
Cholesterol	7.6mg
Sodium	61.4mg
Carbohydrates	20.4g
Protein	7.5g

Ingredients

8 tbsp extra-virgin olive oil, divided
2 lbs. Brussels sprouts, trimmed, halved
lengthwise
6 garlic cloves, chopped
1 C. low sodium chicken broth

1 (15 oz.) cans cannellini, drained
2 tbsp butter
1 C. grated pecorino cheese

Directions

1. Place a large pan over medium heat. Heat in it 3 tbsp of oil.
2. Stir in it 1 lb. of brussels sprouts and cook them for 6 min while stirring often.
3. Drain them and transfer them to a mixing bowl.
4. Repeat the process with another 3 tbsp of oil and the remaining brussels sprouts.
5. Heat 2 tbsp of oil in the same pan Fry in it the garlic on high heat for 60 sec while stirring.
6. Stir in the cooked brussels sprouts with broth.
7. Cook them for 4 min. Stir in the butter with beans. Cook them for 2 min while stirring.
8. Adjust the seasoning of your stir fry then serve it warm.
9. Enjoy.

Backyard
Brussel Sprouts

Prep Time: 5 mins
Total Time: 25 mins

Servings per Recipe: 6
Calories   42.2
Fat   2.5g
Cholesterol   0.0mg
Sodium   12.1mg
Carbohydrates   4.4g
Protein   1.5g

Ingredients

1 tbsp olive oil
2 large garlic cloves, minced
3/4 lb. Brussels sprout, trimmed, leaves pulled off, cores quartered
1/8 tsp lemon pepper

1/8 sea salt
1 tsp lemon zest, minced

Directions

1. Place a large saucepan over medium heat. Heat in it the oil.
2. Cook in it the garlic for 40 sec. Lower the heat and stir in the brussels sprouts.
3. Cook them for 10 to 12 min while stirring them often.
4. Once the time is up, stir in 2 tbsp of water and put on the lid. Cook them for 6 min.
5. Stir in the lemon zest with a pinch of salt and pepper. Serve them warm.
6. Enjoy.

LEMONY
Agave Brussel Sprouts

Prep Time: 10 mins
Total Time: 40 mins

Servings per Recipe: 4

Calories	171.4
Fat	14.3g
Cholesterol	0.0mg
Sodium	109.9mg
Carbohydrates	9.8g
Protein	3.4g

Ingredients

1 lb. Brussels sprout, trimmed
1/4 C. extra-virgin olive oil
1/4 C. agave nectar
2 tbsp mustard
2 tbsp minced garlic

1 lemon, juice

Directions

1. Before you do anything, preheat the oven to 350 F.
2. Cover a baking tray with foil. Place it aside.
3. Get a large mixing bowl: Whisk in it the oil with agave, mustard, and garlic.
4. Add the brussels sprouts with a pinch of salt and pepper. Stir them to coat.
5. Spoon the mixture to the tray and bake it for 15 min.
6. Flip the brussels sprouts and bake them for an extra 15 min.
7. Drizzle over them the lemon juice then serve them warm.
8. Enjoy.

Waldorf
Brussel Sprouts

Prep Time: 10 mins
Total Time: 20 mins

Servings per Recipe: 4

Calories	130.8
Fat	8.9 g
Cholesterol	3.6mg
Sodium	181.5mg
Carbohydrates	9.5g
Protein	5.9g

Ingredients

1 lb. Brussels sprout, trimmed and quartered
2 tsp walnut oil
1 garlic clove, minced
4 tbsp vegetable broth
1/8 tsp salt

1/8 tsp grated nutmeg
pepper
1/4 C. chopped walnuts
1/4 C. grated Parmigiano-Reggiano cheese

Directions

1. Place a large pan over medium heat. Heat in it the oil.

2. Cook in it the sprouts, garlic, salt, nutmeg and pepper for 3 min.

3. Stir in the broth and cook them for 8 to 9 min until it evaporates.

4. Add the walnuts with a pinch of salt and pepper.

5. Transfer them to a serving dish and top them with cheese.

6. Enjoy.

FULL
Barcelona Ceviche

Prep Time: 10 mins
Total Time: 4 hrs 10 mins

Servings per Recipe: 8
Calories	122.7
Fat	2.8g
Cholesterol	130.6mg
Sodium	340.1mg
Carbohydrates	8.7g
Protein	16.1g

Ingredients

1/2 lb. shrimp, peeled and deveined
1/2 lb. squid, cleaned and sliced into rings
1/2 lb. scallops, quartered if large
1 (10 oz.) cans Rotel Tomatoes, drained
2 medium ripe tomatoes, seeded and diced
1/2 large cucumber, peeled and diced
1/2 large green pepper, diced
1/2 medium red sweet onion, diced
1/2 C. chopped fresh cilantro
1 tsp minced garlic
3/4 C. lime juice

1/2 tsp cumin
1 tbsp capers, chopped
1/2 C. hot and spicy hot V8
1 tbsp extra virgin olive oil
1 tsp Accent seasoning
salt & pepper

Directions

1. Place a large saucepan of salted water over high heat. Bring it to a boil.
2. Cook in it the shrimp for 1 min. Drain it and place it in a bowl of ice-cold water.
3. Drain it and chop it. Place it aside.
4. Cook the squid in the same saucepan for 10 sec. Drain it, stir it into the cold water and drain it again.
5. Repeat the process with scallops cooking them for 60 sec.
6. Get a mixing bowl: Stir in it the scallops with shrimp, squid, and lime juice.
7. Cover the bowl and place it in the fridge for 60 min.
8. Once the time is up, stir the remaining ingredients into the seafood bowl. Toss them to coat.
9. Chill it in the fridge for 4 h then serve it.
10. Enjoy.

Catalina's
Cabbage Ceviche

🍳 Prep Time: 10 mins
🕐 Total Time: 30 mins

Servings per Recipe: 12
Calories	108.7
Fat	1.0g
Cholesterol	79.6mg
Sodium	378.1mg
Carbohydrates	15.8g
Protein	11.3g

Ingredients

1 head green cabbage, shredded
6 small English cucumbers, shredded
1 large onion,
1 yellow pepper, shredded
4 large garlic cloves, crushed and mashed with 1 tsp. salt

4 tomatoes, seeded and chopped
4 large limes, juice
1 C. cilantro,
salt and pepper
1 lb. shrimp, peeled and deveined

Directions

1. Bring a large saucepan of water to a boil. Cook in it the shrimp for 2 min.
2. Drain it and chop it.
3. Get a baking dish: Stir in it all the ingredients including the chopped shrimp.
4. cover the bowl and place it in the fridge for 30 min. Serve it with some chips.
5. Enjoy.

CEVICHE
Brasileiro

Prep Time: 1 hr
Total Time: 1 hr 15 mins

Servings per Recipe: 6

Calories	544.1
Fat	31.4g
Cholesterol	92.9mg
Sodium	132.4mg
Carbohydrates	13.0g
Protein	53.5g

Ingredients

3 lbs. flank steaks
6 oz. mixed baby greens
Ceviche
2 lbs. button mushrooms
1/3 C. squeezed lemon juice
1/2 C. squeezed lime juice
1/3 C. squeezed orange juice
1/3 C. olive oil

1 red onion, sliced
1 red bell pepper, seeded, sliced
4 cloves garlic, minced
2 tbsp chopped cilantro
salt and pepper

Directions

1. Get a mixing bowl: Stir in it the mushrooms, lemon juice, orange juice, lime juice and olive oil.
2. Cover the bowl and let it sit for 60 min.
3. Once the time is up, stir in the onion, bell pepper, garlic, cilantro, salt, and pepper.
4. Cover it and let it sit in the fridge for 3 hours at least.
5. Before you do anything else, preheat the grill and grease it.
6. Season the steak with a pinch of salt and pepper. Cook it on the grill for 7 to 9 min on each side.
7. Serve it warm with the ceviche.
8. Enjoy.

Country Ceviche

🥣 Prep Time: 30 mins
🕐 Total Time: 40 mins

Servings per Recipe: 8
Calories   144.7
Fat   1.0g
Cholesterol   0.0mg
Sodium   310.6mg
Carbohydrates   32.1g
Protein   6.2g

Ingredients

3 ears sweet corn
2 - 4 garlic cloves, minced
1 (14 1/2 oz.) cans black beans, rinsed and drained
4 - 5 limes, zested and juiced
2 celery ribs, diced
1 cucumber, diced
3 tomatoes, diced
1/2 C. cilantro, chopped
1 - 2 jalapeno, diced

1/2 red onion, diced
1 red bell pepper, diced
1 green bell pepper, diced
1 yellow bell pepper, diced
1 C. pineapple, chopped
1 C. mango, chopped
1 tsp salt

Directions

1. Scrap off the kernels from the cob.
2. Place a skillet over high heat. Heat in it 1 tbsp of olive oil.
3. Cook in it the corn with garlic for 1 to 2 min. Stir in the black beans with lime juice and zest.
4. Get a mixing bowl: Stir in it the remaining ingredients with corn mix, a pinch of salt and pepper.
5. Adjust the seasoning of your ceviche then serve it with some tortilla chips.
6. Enjoy.

SOUTHWEST
Ceviche

Prep Time: 15 mins
Total Time: 4 hrs 15 mins

Servings per Recipe: 4
Calories	390.2
Fat	11.1g
Cholesterol	165.3mg
Sodium	216.5mg
Carbohydrates	5.7g
Protein	64.1g

Ingredients

4 skinned salmon fillets, shredded
4 limes, juice
2 red chilies
2 tbsp coriander, chopped
1/4 tsp ground cumin

2 garlic cloves
4 cm grated fresh ginger

Directions

1. Get a mixing bowl: Stir in it the salmon with tomatoes, green pepper, celery, onion, cilantro, a pinch of salt and pepper.
2. Press the ginger to squeeze out its juice and over the fish mix.
3. Cover the bowl with a plastic wrap and chill it in the fridge for 5 h.
4. Once the time is up, serve your ceviche with some chips.
5. Enjoy.

Bethany Beach
Ceviche

Prep Time: 6 hrs
Total Time: 6 hrs

Servings per Recipe: 6
Calories	85.8
Fat	4.9g
Cholesterol	0.0mg
Sodium	23.6mg
Carbohydrates	12.2g
Protein	1.6g

Ingredients

1 lb. fish, diced
3 limes, juice
2 tomatoes, chopped, remove seeds and juice
1 large green pepper, chopped
3 celery ribs, chopped
1 onion, chopped
1 bunch cilantro
Dressing
2 tbsp olive oil

2 limes, juice of
2 jalapenos, minced, remove seeds and ribs
2 garlic cloves,
1 tsp cayenne pepper
3/4 tsp cumin
salt and pepper

Directions

1. Get a mixing bowl: Stir in it the fish with lime juice. Cover it and let it sit in the fridge for 5 h.
2. Once the time is up, drain the fish and transfer it to a mixing bowl.
3. Stir into it the tomatoes, green pepper, celery, onion, and cilantro. Spoon it into a serving plate.
4. Get a mixing bowl: Whisk in it the dressing ingredients. Drizzle it over the ceviche then serve it.
5. Enjoy.

CINCO DE MAYO
Chili

Prep Time: 10 mins
Total Time: 30 mins

Servings per Recipe: 6
Calories	411 kcal
Fat	17.2 g
Carbohydrates	46.8g
Protein	25.1 g
Cholesterol	57 mg
Sodium	1039 mg

Ingredients

1/4 C. Mazola(R) Corn Oil
1 lb. ground turkey
1 C. diced onion
1 tsp minced garlic
2 tbsp chili powder
1 tbsp ground cumin
1 tbsp chicken-flavored bouillon powder
1 (15 oz.) can black beans, rinsed and drained

1 (11 oz.) can Mexi-corn, drained
1 (12 oz.) package frozen diced butternut squash, thawed
1 (28 oz.) can crushed tomatoes
1 C. water
1/3 C. ketchup
Garnishes:
Shredded Mexican cheese, fresh cilantro, lime wedges, avocado slice

Directions

1. In a large pan, heat the oil on medium heat and stir fry the turkey for about 5-7 minutes, breaking apart.
2. Add the onions, garlic, chili powder, cumin and bouillon powder and cook for about 3-5 minutes.
3. Stir in the vegetables, tomatoes, water and ketchup and bring to a boil.
4. Reduce the heat to low and simmer for about 10 minutes.
5. Serve with a topping of the desired garnishing.

Saturday Night
Texan Rice

🥣 Prep Time: 10 mins

🕐 Total Time: 40 mins

Servings per Recipe: 6

Calories	177.0
Fat	5.2g
Cholesterol	0.0mg
Sodium	295.9mg
Carbohydrates	27.8g
Protein	4.1g

Ingredients

2 cloves peeled and halved garlic

2 tbsp vegetable oil

1 C. long grain white rice (not instant or fast cooking)

1 (14 1/2 oz.) cans chicken broth

1/4 C. salsa

1/4 C. chopped diced carrot

1/4 C. frozen corn

Directions

1. In a heavy pan, heat the oil on high heat and cook the garlic till browned, stirring occasionally.

2. Remove the garlic cloves from the pan.

3. Add the rice into the garlic oil and reduce the heat to medium-high.

4. Cook, stirring constantly till the rice become brown.

5. Add broth, salsa, carrots and corn and reduce the heat to low.

6. Cook, covered for about 20 minutes.

7. With a fork, fluff the rice before serving.

TRADITIONAL
Mexican Spicy Vermicelli

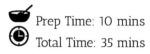 Prep Time: 10 mins
Total Time: 35 mins

Servings per Recipe: 4
Calories	311.6
Fat	7.9g
Cholesterol	0.0mg
Sodium	891.6mg
Carbohydrates	51.7g
Protein	9.2g

Ingredients

2 tbsp vegetable oil
1 medium onion, chopped
2 garlic cloves, minced
8 oz. vermicelli, broken up, 2 C.
1 tsp salt
1/2 tsp pepper

1/2 tsp cumin
1 (4 oz.) cans green chilies, chopped
1 (8 oz.) cans tomato sauce
2 C. water

Directions

1. In a wide skillet, heat the oil on medium heat and cook the onion for about 10 minutes, stirring occasionally.

2. Add the garlic and cook for about 1-2 minutes.

3. Break the vermicelli into 2-inches pieces and add into the skillet.

4. Cook for about 3-4 minutes, stirring occasionally.

5. Add the salt, pepper, cumin, green chilies, tomato sauce and water and bring to a boil on high heat.

6. Reduce the heat to low and simmer, covered for about 10 minutes.

Mexican
Cheese Dumplings

🥣 Prep Time: 20 mins
🕐 Total Time: 36 mins

Servings per Recipe: 6
Calories	386 kcal
Fat	16.4 g
Carbohydrates	40.2g
Protein	18 g
Cholesterol	50 mg
Sodium	2322 mg

Ingredients

2 links chorizo sausage, cut into small pieces
1/2 C. part-skim ricotta cheese
1 C. shredded queso asadero (white Mexican cheese)
1/2 C. chopped cilantro
1 clove garlic, finely minced
1/2 tsp cumin

1 tsp salt
1 (14 oz.) package round wonton wrappers
1 tsp olive oil
1 tbsp salt

Directions

1. Heat a large skillet on medium heat and cook the chorizo till cooked completely.
2. Remove from the heat and keep aside to cool.
3. In a large bowl, mix together the ricotta, queso asadero, cilantro, garlic, cumin and salt.
4. For the filling in a food processor, add the chorizo and pulse till grounded finely.
5. Add the ricotta mixture in the blender and pulse till well combined.
6. Place a tspful of the filling in the center of a wonton wrapper.
7. With a wet finger, moisten the top half edge of the wrapper.
8. Fold in the half and pinch the edges to seal.
9. Repeat with the the remaining wrappers and filling.
10. In a pan of the boiling water, add the oil and about 1 tbsp of the salt.
11. Gently place raviolis into the water and cook for about 6 minutes.
12. With a slotted spoon, transfer onto a serving platter.
13. Serve with a topping of the marinara sauce.

MEXICO CITY
-San Antonio Pierogies

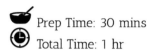 Prep Time: 30 mins

Total Time: 1 hr

Servings per Recipe: 6
Calories	561.4
Fat	33.3g
Cholesterol	230.5mg
Sodium	945.7mg
Carbohydrates	16.1g
Protein	13.3g

Ingredients

For The Dough
2 C. flour
1 egg (beaten)
1/2 tsp salt
1/4 C. butter (cold and cubed)
1/2 C. sour cream
For The Filling
1 lb ground turkey
1/2 C. finely diced onion
2 minced garlic cloves
1/4 C. corn kernel (frozen)
3 chipotle peppers, minced
2 tbsp of the adobo sauce
1/4 tsp salt
1/2 tsp paprika

1/4 tsp cumin
1/4 tsp cayenne
1 C. chicken stock
2 C. Simply Potatoes Traditional Mashed
Potatoes
1/2 C. colby-monterey jack cheese
2 - 3 tbsp melted butter
For The Dipping Sauce
1 C. sour cream
3 tbsp taco seasoning
1 tbsp chopped green onion

Directions

1. For the dough in a food processor, pulse the flour and salt and pulse to break up any lumps.
2. Add the beaten egg and pulse 2-3 times.
3. Add the sour cream and butter and pulse for about 5-6 times.
4. Place the dough onto a smooth surface and shape into a ball.
5. In a plastic wrap, wrap the dough and refrigerate for at least 20 minutes.
6. For filling, heat a pan and cook the turkey till browned and then start breaking apart the meat.
7. Stir in the chopped onions, salt, paprika, cumin and cayenne and cook till the onions become softened.

8. Stir in the corn and chipotle peppers and garlic and cook for about 1 minute.
9. Stir in the Adobo Sauce and 1/4 C. of the chicken stock and cook, stirring till almost all the liquid is absorbed.
10. Add 1/4 C. of the chicken stock and cook, stirring till almost all the liquid is absorbed.
11. Now, add the remaining 1/2 C. of the chicken stock and cook, stirring till most of the liquid is absorbed.
12. Remove from the heat and keep aside to cool.
13. In a bowl, mix together the Simply Potatoes Mashed Potatoes and cheese.
14. Divide the dough into 1-inch balls and dust with the flour.
15. Place the dough onto a floured surface and roll into 3-4 inch rounds.
16. In the middle of each round, place a spoon full of the potato mixture, followed by a spoonful of the taco filling.
17. Fold in half and press together at the top.
18. Seal the edges tightly with wet fingers.
19. Arrange on a floured sheet pan.
20. In a pan of salted boiling water, cook 6-8 Pierogies at a time for about 8-10 minutes.
21. Remove from the pan and keep aside to cool slightly.
22. Coat with the melted butter on one side.
23. In a hot skillet, place the pierogies, buttered side down and cook till crisp.
24. Coat the tops with the butter and flip the side and cook till crisp.
25. For the dipping sauce in a bowl, mix together the sour cream, chopped green onion and taco seasoning.
26. Arrange the Pierogies on a platter with the dipping sauce and serve with a sprinkling of green onion.

SAN LUIS
Salmon

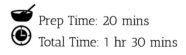

Prep Time: 20 mins
Total Time: 1 hr 30 mins

Servings per Recipe: 4
Calories	394 kcal
Fat	21.6 g
Carbohydrates	11.9g
Protein	38.2 g
Cholesterol	119 mg
Sodium	298 mg

Ingredients

2 tbsp olive oil
2 limes, juiced
2 marinated roasted red peppers, with liquid
1 clove garlic, finely chopped
1/8 tsp ground allspice
1/8 tsp ground cinnamon
1/4 tsp ground cumin
1/4 tsp white sugar
salt and pepper to taste

1 1/2 lb. salmon steaks
1 large tomato, cut into thin wedges
3 green onions, chopped
1 C. shredded lettuce
1 lime, sliced

Directions

1. In a large nonreactive bowl, mix together the olive oil, juice of the 2 limes, roasted red peppers, garlic, allspice, cinnamon, cumin, sugar, salt and pepper.
2. Add the salmon steaks and rub with the mixture evenly.
3. Refrigerate, covered for at least 1 hour.
4. Set the broiler of your oven.
5. In a broiler pan, place the salmon steaks in a single layer.
6. Cook under the broiler for about 3-5 minutes per side.
7. In a small bowl, mix together the tomato wedges and green onions.
8. Serve salmon with the tomato mixture, lettuce and lime wedges.

Caribbean x Mexican Chuck Roast

🥣 Prep Time: 30 mins
🕐 Total Time: 16 hrs 40 mins

Servings per Recipe: 24
Calories   175 kcal
Fat   12.5 g
Carbohydrates   1.2g
Protein   13.5 g
Cholesterol   52 mg
Sodium   34 mg

Ingredients

4 dried guajillo chilies
2 tsp cumin seeds
1/8 whole cloves
1 C. boiling water
1/2 tsp ground ancho chili powder
1 large onion, quartered
6 cloves garlic

2 tsp dried oregano
1 tsp ground thyme
1/3 C. apple cider vinegar
2 tsp lime juice
1 (6 lb.) boneless beef chuck roast
2 bay leaves

Directions

1. Heat a heavy skillet on medium heat and cook the dried guajillo chilis for about 5 minutes, turning occasionally.
2. Remove from the heat and keep aside to cool for a moment.
3. Meanwhile in a hot skillet, toast the cumin and cloves. Remove from the pan and keep aside.
4. Remove and discard the stems, seeds and veins of the chilis and place into a small bowl.
5. Place the boiling water over top and keep aside, covered for about 1 hour.
6. Grind the toasted cumin and cloves into a powder form.
7. Remove the chilis from the soaking water, and place into the blender along with 1/3 C. of the soaking liquid, ancho chili powder, onion, garlic, oregano, thyme, vinegar, lime juice, powdered cumin and cloves and pulse till a smooth paste forms.
8. In a bowl, add the guajillo chili paste. Add the beef roast and coat with the paste evenly. With a plastic wrap, cover the bowl and refrigerate to marinate for overnight.
9. Set your oven to 325 degrees F. In a roasting pan, place the roast and marinade and top with the bay leaves. With a foil paper, cover tightly and cook in the oven for about 6 hours. Remove from the oven and keep aside, covered at the room temperature for about 1 hour. Discard the bay leaves and shred with two forks before serving

REAL
Authentic Tamales

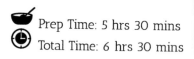

Prep Time: 5 hrs 30 mins
Total Time: 6 hrs 30 mins

Servings per Recipe: 36
Calories	347 kcal
Fat	24.4 g
Carbohydrates	23.3g
Protein	9.1 g
Cholesterol	38 mg
Sodium	248 mg

Ingredients

4 lb. boneless chuck roast
4 cloves garlic
3 (8 oz.) packages dried corn husks
4 dried ancho chilis
2 tbsp vegetable oil
2 tbsp all-purpose flour
1 C. beef broth
1 tsp cumin seeds
1 tsp ground cumin
2 cloves garlic, minced

2 tsp chopped fresh oregano
1 tsp red pepper flakes
1 tsp white vinegar
salt to taste
3 C. lard
1 tbsp salt
9 C. masa harina

Directions

1. In a large pan, add the beef, garlic and enough cold water to cover on high heat and bring to a boil.
2. Reduce the heat and simmer, covered for about 3 1/2 hours.
3. Remove the beef from the pan and keep aside to cool, then shred it.
4. Reserve 5 C. of the cooking liquid and discard the garlic.
5. Meanwhile, in a large container, place the corn husks and cover with the warm water.
6. Place an inverted plate and a heavy can to weight down and keep aside for about 3 hours.
7. In a cast iron skillet, toast the ancho chilis.
8. Keep aside to cool and then remove the stems and seeds.
9. Crumble and grind in a clean coffee grinder.
10. In a large skillet, heat the oil.
11. Add the flour and cook, stirring till browned slightly.
12. Add about 1 C. of the beef broth and stir till smooth.
13. Add the shredded beef, ground chilis, cumin seeds, ground cumin, minced garlic, oregano,

red pepper flakes, vinegar and salt.

14. Simmer, covered for about 45 minutes.
15. In a large bowl, add the lard and salt and with an electric mixer, beat on high speed till fluffy.
16. Add the masa harina and beat at low speed till well combined.
17. Slowly, add the reserved cooking liquid and beating contiguously till mixture becomes like a soft cookie dough.
18. Drain water from the corn husks.
19. One at a time, flatten out each husk, with the narrow end facing you.
20. Spread about 2 tbsp of the masa mixture onto the top 2/3 of the husk.
21. Spread about 1 tbsp of meat mixture down the middle of the masa.
22. Roll up the corn husk starting at one of the long sides.
23. Fold the narrow end of the husk onto the rolled tamale and tie with a piece of butchers' twine.
24. In a steamer basket, place the tamales and steam over boiling water for about 1 hour.
25. Serve immediately.

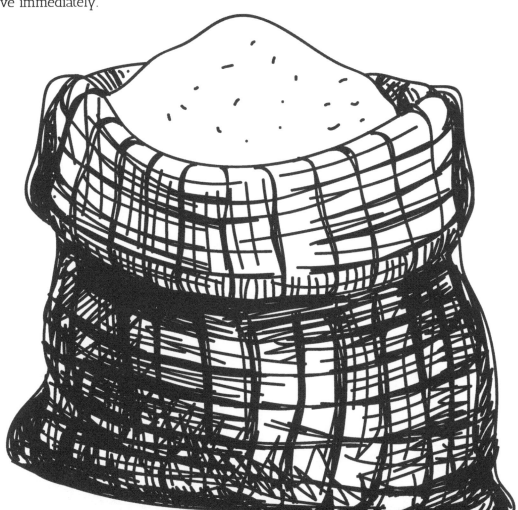

FRESH GREEN
Enchiladas

Prep Time: 10 mins
Total Time: 30 mins

Servings per Recipe: 4	
Calories	559 kcal
Fat	25 g
Carbohydrates	48.9g
Protein	37.1 g
Cholesterol	84 mg
Sodium	1344 mg

Ingredients

2 bone-in chicken breast halves
2 C. chicken broth
1/4 white onion
1 clove garlic
2 tsp salt
1 lb. fresh tomatillos, husks removed
5 serrano peppers
1/4 white onion
1 clove garlic
1 pinch salt

12 corn tortillas
1/4 C. vegetable oil
1 C. crumbled queso fresco
1/2 white onion, chopped
1 bunch fresh cilantro, chopped

Directions

1. In a pan, mix together the chicken breast, broth, 1/4 of the onion, 1 garlic clove and 2 tsp of the salt and bring to a boil.
2. Boil for about 20 minutes.
3. Transfer the chicken into a plate and keep aside to cool.
4. Strain the broth and reserve it.
5. Discard the onion and garlic.
6. After cooling, shred the chicken.
7. In a pan, add the tomatillos and serrano chilis with enough water to cover and bring to a boil.
8. Boil till the tomatillos turn into a dull army green color.
9. Strain the tomatillos mixture and transfer in a blender.
10. Add reserved broth, 1/4 of the onion, 1 garlic clove and a pinch of salt and pulse till pureed finely.
11. Transfer the salsa in a medium pan and bring to a gentle simmer.

12. In a frying pan, heat the oil and fry the tortillas, one by one.

13. Transfer the tortillas on a paper towel to drain.

14. Dip the slightly fried tortillas in low-boiling green salsa slightly.

15. Divide the tortillas into the serving plates.

16. Top the tortillas with the shredded chicken, followed by the extra green sauce, crumbled cheese, chopped onion and chopped cilantro.

RED, WHITE,
and Green Soup

🥣 Prep Time: 30 mins
🕐 Total Time: 8 hrs 30 mins

Servings per Recipe: 8
Calories	225 kcal
Fat	5.3 g
Carbohydrates	31.8g
Protein	14.3 g
Cholesterol	139 mg
Sodium	1679 mg

Ingredients

3 gallons water, divided
2 1/2 lb. beef tripe, cut into 1-inch pieces
6 cloves garlic, finely chopped
1 large white onion, finely chopped
1 1/2 tbsp salt
1 tbsp ground black pepper
1 1/2 tbsp dried oregano

2 tbsp ground red pepper
5 de arbol chili peppers
6 japones chili peppers, seeds removed
6 C. canned white hominy, drained
1/2 white onion, chopped
1/4 C. chopped fresh cilantro
2 limes, juiced

Directions

1. In a large pan, bring 1 gallon water to a boil and add the tripe.
2. Reduce the heat and simmer for about 2 hours.
3. With a spoon, skim off the fat occasionally.
4. Drain the water and add a fresh gallon of the water.
5. Simmer for about 2 hours. Drain well.
6. Add the remaining 1 gallon water in the pan with tripe and bring to a boil.
7. Stir in the garlic, 1 white onion, salt, pepper, oregano and red pepper.
8. Reduce heat and simmer for about 1 hour. Set the broiler of your oven.
9. Place the de arbol chili peppers on a baking sheet and cook under the broiler for about 2 minutes.
10. Remove from the oven and slit lengthwise, then remove the seeds.
11. In a food processor, add the de arbol chili peppers and japones chili peppers and pulse till chopped finely.
12. Add the pepper mixture into the pan and cook for about 2 hours on low heat.
13. Stir in the hominy and cook for about 1 hour.
14. Serve with the remaining onion, cilantro and lime juice.

Tampico
Inspired Meal Pie

Prep Time: 30 mins
Total Time: 1 hr

Servings per Recipe: 16

Calories	432 kcal
Fat	23.9 g
Carbohydrates	33.3g
Protein	19.8 g
Cholesterol	68 mg
Sodium	847 mg

Ingredients

2 lb. ground beef
1 onion, chopped
2 tsp minced garlic
1 (2 oz.) can black olives, sliced
1 (4 oz.) can diced green chili peppers
1 (10 oz.) can diced tomatoes with green chili peppers
1 (16 oz.) jar taco sauce

2 (16 oz.) cans refried beans
12 (8 inch) flour tortillas
9 oz. shredded Colby cheese

Directions

1. Set your oven to 350 degrees F before doing anything else.
2. Heat a large skillet on medium heat and cook the beef for about 5 minutes.
3. Add the onion and garlic, and sauté for about 5 minutes.
4. Drain any excess fat.
5. Stir in the olives, green chili peppers, tomatoes with green chili peppers, taco sauce and refried beans and reduce the heat to low.
6. Simmer for about 15-20 minutes.
7. In the bottom of a large casserole dish, place a thin layer of the beef mixture.
8. Top with a layer of the tortillas, followed by the beef mixture and a layer of the cheese.
9. Repeat the layers till all the ingredients are used.
10. Cook in the oven for about 20-30 minutes.

SPICY
Honey Tilapia Tacos

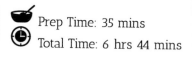

Prep Time: 35 mins
Total Time: 6 hrs 44 mins

Servings per Recipe: 6
Calories	416 kcal
Fat	19.2 g
Carbohydrates	38.5g
Protein	22.6 g
Cholesterol	43 mg
Sodium	644 mg

Ingredients

Marinade
1/4 C. extra virgin olive oil
2 tbsp distilled white vinegar
2 tbsp fresh lime juice
2 tsp lime zest
1 1/2 tsp honey
2 cloves garlic, minced
1/2 tsp cumin
1/2 tsp chili powder
1 tsp seafood seasoning
1/2 tsp ground black pepper
1 tsp hot pepper sauce
1 lb. tilapia fillets, cut into chunks
Dressing
1 (8 oz.) container light sour cream
1/2 C. adobo sauce from chipotle

peppers
2 tbsp fresh lime juice
2 tsp lime zest
1/4 tsp cumin
1/4 tsp chili powder
1/2 tsp seafood seasoning
salt and pepper to taste
Toppings
1 (10 oz.) package tortillas
3 ripe tomatoes, seeded and diced
1 bunch cilantro, chopped
1 small head cabbage, cored and shredded
2 limes, cut in wedges

Directions

1. For marinade in a bowl, add the olive oil, vinegar, lime juice, lime zest, honey, garlic, cumin, chili powder, seafood seasoning, black pepper and hot sauce and beat till well combined.
2. In a shallow dish, add the tilapia and marinade and mix. Refrigerate, covered for about 6 - 8 hours.
3. For the dressing in a bowl, mix together the sour cream and adobo sauce..
4. Stir in the lime juice, lime zest, cumin, chili powder, seafood seasoning, salt and pepper.
5. Refrigerate, covered till serving.
6. Set your outdoor grill for high heat and lightly, grease the grill grate.

7. Arrange the grill grate 4-inch from the heat.
8. Remove the tilapia from marinade and discard off any excess marinade.
9. Cook the tilapia on the grill for about 9 minutes, flipping once in the middle way.
10. For the tacos, place the tilapia pieces in the center of each tortilla with the desired amounts of tomatoes, cilantro, and cabbage.
11. Top with the dressing.
12. Roll up the tortillas around the fillings and serve with a garnishing of the lime wedges.

MEXICAN
Skillet

🥣 Prep Time: 20 mins
🕐 Total Time: 30 mins

Servings per Recipe: 4
Calories	212 kcal
Fat	4.6 g
Carbohydrates	36.8g
Protein	10.1 g
Cholesterol	0 mg
Sodium	818 mg

Ingredients

1 tbsp olive oil
1 large onion, chopped
3 cloves garlic, minced
4 small zucchini, diced
1 fresh poblano chili pepper, seeded and chopped

1 C. frozen whole kernel corn
1 (15 oz.) can black beans, rinsed and drained
1/2 tsp salt

Directions

1. In a large skillet, heat the oil on medium-high heat and sauté the onion and garlic till tender.
2. Add the zucchini and poblano pepper, and sauté till soft.
3. Stir in the corn and beans and cook till heated completely.
4. Season with the salt to taste

Chipotle Veggies & Black-Eyed Peas

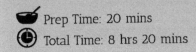

Prep Time: 20 mins

Total Time: 8 hrs 20 mins

Servings per Recipe: 20

Calories	165 kcal
Fat	2.7 g
Carbohydrates	26.9 g
Protein	9.2 g
Cholesterol	0 mg
Sodium	170 mg

Ingredients

2 tbsps olive oil
1 tbsp balsamic vinegar
1 C. chopped orange bell pepper
1 C. chopped celery
1 C. chopped carrot
1 C. chopped onion
1 tsp minced garlic
2 (16 oz.) packages dry black-eyed peas
4 C. water
4 tsps vegetable bouillon base (such as
Better Than Bouillon(R) Vegetable Base)

1 (7 oz.) can chipotle peppers in adobo sauce,
chopped, sauce reserved
2 tsps liquid mesquite smoke flavoring
2 tsps ground cumin
1/2 tsp ground black pepper

Directions

1. In a skillet, heat the vinegar and oil and sauté the onion, celery, bell pepper and carrot for about 5-8 minutes.
2. In a slow cooker, transfer the vegetable mixture with the remaining ingredients and stir to combine.
3. Set the slow cooker to Low and cook, covered for about 8 hours.

CHEESY
Chipotle Lamb Burgers in Maple Glaze

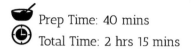 Prep Time: 40 mins

Total Time: 2 hrs 15 mins

Servings per Recipe: 4	
Calories	609 kcal
Fat	33.7 g
Carbohydrates	42g
Protein	33.5 g
Cholesterol	110 mg
Sodium	1482 mg

Ingredients

1 head garlic
1 pound ground lamb
6 oz. soft goat cheese
6 tbsps minced chipotle peppers in adobo sauce
2 sprigs chopped fresh rosemary
2 tbsps maple syrup

1 1/2 tsps salt
1/2 tsp cracked black pepper
1 tbsp olive oil
2 tbsps maple syrup
4 ciabatta buns, split and toasted

Directions

1. Set your oven to 300 degrees F before doing anything else.
2. Cut the top of the garlic head and arrange it in a small baking dish and cook it in the oven for about 1 hour or till golden brown.
3. Remove everything from the oven and let it cool completely.
4. In a bowl, squeeze the garlic head completely.
5. Add the lamb, 2 tbsps of maple syrup, goat cheese, chipotle peppers, rosemary, salt and black pepper and mix till well combined and make 4 equal sized patties from the mixture.
6. In a large skillet, heat the oil on medium-high heat and cook the patties for about 1 minute per side.
7. Reduce the heat to medium-low and cook the patties for about 2 minutes per side or till the desired doneness.
8. Just before the last minute of cooking, add the remaining maple syrup.
9. Serve these patties in the buns.

Hot
Chipotle Peach Salsa

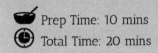 Prep Time: 10 mins

Total Time: 20 mins

Servings per Recipe: 4
Calories	41 kcal
Fat	0.1 g
Carbohydrates	10.3g
Protein	0.8 g
Cholesterol	0 mg
Sodium	17 mg

Ingredients

1 C. sliced canned peaches, drained and chopped
1/3 C. chopped red onion
2 cloves garlic, minced
1 1/2 tsps minced fresh ginger root
2 tsps minced chipotle peppers in adobo sauce

1/3 C. chopped fresh cilantro
1/2 lime, juiced
salt and pepper to taste

Directions

1. In a large bowl, add all the ingredients and mix till well combined.
2. Refrigerate to chill before serving.

BEEF BRISKET
in Chipotle Gravy

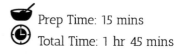

Prep Time: 15 mins
Total Time: 1 hr 45 mins

Servings per Recipe: 6

Calories	809 kcal
Fat	65.4 g
Carbohydrates	112.9 g
Protein	39.6 g
Cholesterol	164 mg
Sodium	1593 mg

Ingredients

2 (11 oz.) cans whole tomatillos, drained
1 (7 oz.) can chipotle peppers in adobo sauce
1 (8 oz.) can tomato sauce
1 C. water
2 tsps salt
1 tsp brown sugar

2 tbsps olive oil
1 yellow onion, chopped
4 cloves garlic, chopped
1 (3 pound) beef brisket

Directions

1. In a food processor, add chipotle peppers, tomatillos, tomato sauce, brown sugar, water and salt and pulse till smooth.
2. In a pressure cooker, heat oil on medium heat and sauté the onion and garlic for about 3 minutes.
3. Add the brisket and sear on both sides.
4. Stir in the chipotle mixture and bring to a boil.
5. Cover the pressure cooker with a lid and bring to medium pressure on high heat.
6. Reduce the heat to low and cook on medium pressure for about 1 hour and 15 minutes.
7. Turn off the heat and release the pressure by the method of natural release.
8. Serve the brisket with the pan sauce.

Classic
Teriyaki Sauce

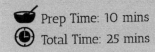 Prep Time: 10 mins
Total Time: 25 mins

Servings per Recipe: 1
Calories   133.4
Fat   0.0g
Cholesterol   0.0mg
Sodium   2062.3mg
Carbohydrates   30.1g
Protein   4.0g

Ingredients

1/4 C. tamari soy sauce
1 C. water
freshly grated ginger
3 tbsps brown sugar
1 minced garlic clove

2 tbsps cornstarch
1/4 C. cold water

Directions

1. Place a saucepan over medium heat. Stir in it 1 C. water, tamari, brown sugar, garlic, and ginger.
2. Cook them until they start boiling while stirring all the time.
3. Get a mixing bowl: Whisk in it the cornstarch with 1/4 C. of water.
4. Add it to the saucepan and keep whisking it until it becomes thick.
5. Adjust the seasoning of your teriyaki sauce then serve it.
6. Enjoy.

CLASSIC
Teriyaki Chuck Burgers

Prep Time: 15 mins
Total Time: 25 mins

Servings per Recipe: 6
Calories	517.5
Fat	27.7g
Cholesterol	104.3mg
Sodium	1157.1mg
Carbohydrates	34.1g
Protein	31.7g

Ingredients

1/4 C. soy sauce
1/4 C. honey
2 cloves garlic, pressed
1 tsp ginger
1/3 C. mayonnaise
2 lbs. ground chuck
1/2 tsp salt

1/4 tsp pepper
6 hamburger buns

Directions

1. Before you do anything, preheat the grill and grease it.
2. Get a mixing bowl: Whisk in it the soy sauce with honey, garlic, and ginger.
3. Get a small mixing bowl: Whisk in it 2 tsp of the honey mixture with mayo. Place it aside.
4. Add the beef with salt, and pepper to the remaining honey mixture. Mix them well.
5. Shape the mixture into 6 patties. Coat them with a cooking spray.
6. Place them on the grill and let them cook for 3 to 4 min on each side.
7. Assemble your burgers with toppings of your choice then serve them warm.
8. Enjoy.

Teriyaki Chicken Thighs

Prep Time: 15 mins
Total Time: 30 mins

Servings per Recipe: 4

Calories	242.3
Fat	8.2g
Cholesterol	115.0mg
Sodium	1047.3mg
Carbohydrates	11.9g
Protein	28.9g

Ingredients

Marinade
1/4 C. ketchup
1/4 C. hoisin sauce
2 tbsps soy sauce
2 tbsps rice vinegar
2 tsps garlic, minced
2 tsps ginger, minced

2 tsps dark sesame oil
Chicken
8 boneless skinless chicken thighs
sesame seeds, toasted in a skillet
cooked rice
green onion top, cut into strips

Directions

1. Get a mixing bowl: Whisk in it all the marinade ingredients.
2. Place the chicken thighs in a zip lock bag. Pour over it the marinade.
3. Seal the bag and shake it to coat. Let them marinade for 5 h.
4. Before you do anything, preheat the grill and grease it.
5. Drain the chicken thighs and grill them for 6 to 7 min on each side.
6. Garnish them with some sesame seeds and green onion. Serve them warm.
7. Enjoy.

TERIYAKI
Penne

Prep Time: 5 mins
Total Time: 15 mins

Servings per Recipe: 6
Calories   189.1
Fat   3.3g
Cholesterol   0.0mg
Sodium   478.0mg
Carbohydrates   36.2g
Protein   5.6g

Ingredients

8 ounces penne pasta
1/2 tsp grated ginger
1 clove garlic, minced
1 tbsp toasted sesame oil
3 C. broccoli slaw mix

2 C. sliced fresh mushrooms
1/4 C. teriyaki sauce
1/4 C. sliced green onion

Directions

1. Prepare the pasta by following the instructions on the package. Drain it.
2. Place a large pan over medium heat. Heat in it the oil. Cook in it the ginger for 10 sec.
3. Add the broccoli with teriyaki sauce and mushrooms. Season them with a pinch of salt and pepper.
4. Let them cook for 6 min. Add the pasta and stir them to coat.
5. Serve your teriyaki slaw salad warm.
6. Enjoy.

Tropical
Teriyaki Kabobs

Prep Time: 15 mins
Total Time: 20 mins

Servings per Recipe: 4
Calories   931.9
Fat   82.8g
Cholesterol   112.3mg
Sodium   2046.7mg
Carbohydrates   34.4g
Protein   13.8g

Ingredients

1 lb. beef, cubed
1 (16 ounce) cans pineapple chunks in juice
1/2 C. soy sauce
1/4 C. brown sugar
2 garlic cloves, minced
1/2 tsp minced ginger

1/2 tsp sliced lemongrass
1/4 C. sliced scallion
2 tsps sesame oil

Directions

1. Get a large zip lock bag: Place in it all the ingredients and seal it.
2. Shake it to coat them. Place it in the fridge for 3 h.
3. Before you do anything, preheat the grill and grease it.
4. Drain the beef and pineapple chunks from the marinade. Thread them while alternating between them onto skewers.
5. Grill them for 4 to 6 min on each side. Serve them warm.
6. Enjoy.

TERIYAKI
Steak BBQ

Prep Time: 15 mins
Total Time: 25 mins

Servings per Recipe: 6
Calories	238.2
Fat	9.4g
Cholesterol	68.0mg
Sodium	962.5mg
Carbohydrates	9.6g
Protein	28.7g

Ingredients

1/3 C. soy sauce
2 tbsps vegetable oil
1 tbsp brown sugar
1 garlic clove, minced
1 tsp ground ginger
1 tsp seasoning salt
1 1/2 lbs. boneless sirloin steaks, cubed

12 fresh mushrooms
1 large green pepper, cut into pieces
1 large onion, cut into wedges
12 cherry tomatoes

Directions

1. Get a mixing bowl: Mix in it the soy sauce, oil, brown sugar, garlic, ginger, and salt to make the marinade.
2. Get a large zip lock bag. Place in it the beef slices and pour over the marinade.
3. Seal the bag and shake it to coat. Place it in the fridge and let it sit overnight.
4. Before you do anything, preheat the grill and grease it.
5. Drain the beef dices and thread along with cherry tomatoes, green pepper, onion, and mushrooms onto skewers.
6. Grill them for 5 to 7 min on each side while basting them with the remaining marinade.
7. Serve your kabobs warm with some pita bread.
8. Enjoy.

ENJOY THE RECIPES?

KEEP ON COOKING
WITH 6 MORE FREE COOKBOOKS!

Visit our website and simply enter your email address to join the club and receive your 6 cookbooks.

http://booksumo.com/magnet

https://www.instagram.com/booksumopress/

https://www.facebook.com/booksumo/

Printed in Great Britain
by Amazon